POLITICS & DIRTY TRICKS

POLITICS & DIRTY TRICKS

A Guide to Screwing Up the System

V.R. Farb

PALADIN PRESS
BOULDER, COLORADO

Politics and Dirty Tricks:
A Guide to Screwing up the System
by V.R. Farb

Copyright © 1995 by V.R. Farb

ISBN 0-87364-821-8
Printed in the United States of America

Published by Paladin Press, a division of
Paladin Enterprises, Inc., P.O. Box 1307,
Boulder, Colorado 80306, USA.
(303) 443-7250

Direct inquiries and/or orders to the above address.

Contents

Preface

"Aren't you fearful that the other side will use this information to get some of our friends," questioned an otherwise astute political observer recently upon learning that I intended to write a working summary of political action for the 90s.

It's a good question, but who are our friends, and exactly who is on the "other side," aside from greedy, thieving, self-serving politicians?

"My dictionary," I responded, "defines theft as 'the felonious taking and removal of personal property with intent to deprive the rightful owner of it.'" To be sure, some politicians steal less than others, but to the best of my knowledge, all steal.

Authority for the position that taxation is theft comes from fairly lofty sources. The "Good Book," for instance, is abundantly clear about all taxation being theft. Ancient Jews were warned that kings would consume up to 10 percent of each person's private productive capacity. Christ reckoned that no difference existed between tax collectors and prostitutes. We are taught by the Ten Commandments not to steal nor to patronize prostitutes.

"Vote the bastards out of office!" is the plaintive cry. Those who espouse this often laudatory goal fail to realize that a democracy is best described as two wolves and a lamb voting about what to have for lunch.

Powers of incumbency are so great in our system that the prestigious national newspaper *The Wall Street Journal* reckons that turnover in the British House of Lords is greater than in the U.S. House of Representatives and Senate. The British House of Lords is, of course, a hereditary outfit. Our own senators and representatives are supposedly elected by popular vote. But, as a practical matter, few legislators who decide to run for reelection ever fail.

So what is Joe Citizen to do about this well-organized crime syndicate, other than taking the advice of Tevvie from *Fiddler on the Roof* to "stay as far away from the tsar as possible"? Especially when, in this day and age, the tsar intrudes into our every private affair—and one cannot possibly stay far away?

The simple answer includes using tricks, techniques, and devices, many of which rival politicians developed to make life so miserable for the opposing thieves that they would find gainful employment elsewhere. It is generally acknowledged by insiders who should know, for instance, that George Bush whomped Michael Dukakis so heartily in part because Bush's advanced team was extremely adept at throwing a monkey wrench into the gears of the Dukakis machine. In 1989, Willie outslicked old George using similar tactics. The 1989–1990 Democratic primary brought forth a couple who proved they were absolute masters at political intrigue. Their election proved that the tactics which follow can be effective.

Politics and Dirty Tricks is not meant to be a theoretical study. Almost every one of the techniques outlined has been deployed successfully, many by average fed-up citizens. Often one hears about devices for dealing with truly obnoxious people that are totally impractical. It is demonstrably ineffective to suggest that one organize a mass protest rally attended by thousands of people. Even if instructions for that volley were perfect, where does one get his or her cast of thousands?

The trip to this place is rife with pitfalls. Smart monkey wrenchers will help greedy pols fall into the pit.

Most punitive strikes in this business will be made by singular, extremely clever, opportunistic individuals who—with just a little coaching and independent creativity—can make life absolutely miserable for criminals who claim they make decisions for us.

The brief manual that follows is a truncated road map and list of suggestions. When wielded by even half-smart, dedicated people, it will ultimately cause those who wish to make their livings in the most accomplished organized crime syndicate the world has ever known to think again about their actions. At the very least it will make rape and pillage more difficult.

Master politicians claim we always vote against a candidate as opposed to voting for someone. It doesn't matter who or what they are. Any beating back is laudatory at this juncture.

Introduction

We probably agree that politicians have numerous character defects or you wouldn't be reading this manual. But which
of these traits makes pols especially subject to sting techniques that have a tendency to cause them to find urgent
business elsewhere?

Humility, for instance, is never a trait one can find among
politicians. Arrogance characterizes the entire crowd in
Washington. As you go through the following lists of techniques, keep in mind that the only time a politician will ever,
ever say "I am sorry," or "I acted stupidly" is when the polls
suggest that a few extra votes can be wrung from it. Politicians
never want to look as if they're uninformed or not in control.

Even Ross Perot had money problems with his abortive
campaign. Politicians are always strapped for cash. A minimum of $3-5 million is necessary to run for a senate seat in a
small state. Up to $15 million is required in a state such as
California or New York. At the time of this writing, Sen. Diane
Feinstein of California reportedly spent about one-third of
her total time raising money for a campaign still several years
in the future. And for our purposes, wasting or redirecting any

of a politician's scarce and much-needed funds away from the campaign to other uses can have serious consequences.

If successful, most state and national politicians are forced by time and geographics to take up expensive residence in second homes closer to their place of work. They must spend lavishly for reliable transportation, travel, meals away from home, and family expenses such as schooling for their children and expensive clothes. Family security is a constant consideration.

Surprisingly, crime does not pay in this instance. Relatively large salaries do not cover these additional living costs. In this regard, the plaintive cry that "we are getting financially killed working as legislators" has merit.

As a result, these "public servants" face great temptations to misapply any one of a great number of lavish perks to which they are entitled. These include official dinners, paid speaking engagements, and cheap haircuts, dry cleaning, banking, restaurant facilities, parking, mail, telephone usage, and office space, to mention just a very few. Frédéric Bastiat, a 19th-century political philosopher, postulated that a complex government that attempts to regulate in any and all situations will be sufficiently inept that everyone is basically unhappy with the end result, and, more importantly, anyone can always be accused of being a lawbreaker.

Open bribery, because of historic constraints, has not become epidemic in our society. This is in spite of the fact that huge numbers of basic economic decisions are now made by people with no economic basis (politicians). But how else except through bribery is one to get a building permit in most places, avoid the EPA, or be able to open a mine or cut timber on their own property? Instead, we have perfected the institution of near bribes involving rigged business deals wherein politicians are ensured fantastic incomes in exchange for orchestrating political controls. One sage likened it to selling indulgences for sin, common during the Dark Ages. Usually these business deals involve off-the-record, difficult-to-track sums of money.

Politics has come to mean money and power.

While open bribery is not rampant, "exchange" of "walking around money," including wads of 20s, 50s, and 100s, is still common in many parts of the United States. Simply stuffed in a politician's pockets at a reception or a campaign meeting, this is usually only petty cash, not the hundreds of thousands one must use for an effective TV campaign. At best, it represents the next few bottles of booze for a reception. "Walking around money" represents an Achilles' heel for those dealing with politicians. It won't be reported, and anyone who steps forward claiming he provided such will not be regarded by anyone of importance.

Donation of "in kind," such as airplanes, time, stamps, office space and supplies, gasoline, a new car, and so on, which also can be kept off the books, is universal (not traditionally fertile ground on which to dig for slinging-type mud).

More effective is to feed politicians bad information than bad money. They are used to hiding money and perks, but

Our pols will literally trample their mothers' bodies for a seat in the chambers where they speak for thousands.

politicians know they must look like super intelligent whiz kids, always. Find a means of making them look dumb, even now and then, and you really have something.

Throughout this volume, keep in mind that one must look for productive avenues by which politicians can be stung. These are not always obvious, nor are they traditional in terms of how average citizens view politicians.

Henry Kissinger claimed that the only ultimate aphrodisiac is politics. Young women, old Henry said, could not resist the power that goes with the office. All politicians are aware of this truth. Most take advantage of it, but a few, for one reason or another, do not.

However, as President Clinton has demonstrated, this propensity is no longer of political significance to Americans. While one might hope that a politician's tête-à-têtes might provide an opening for attack, they seldom do in this day and age.

Somewhat along this same line of reasoning, politics is very, very hard on families. Few situations develop wherein

If they can win an election, they are, by definition, unfit to serve as legislators.

husband, wife, and children all enjoy the process. In most cases, other family members hate the process through which they are pulled. Divorce, separation, and basket case domestic situations are common. Probably the only exceptions are the Clintons. The Perots managed to escape in one piece as well, but in their case it can be attributed largely to the fact that virtually no one knows or has seen Mrs. Perot. Her name and visual identity remain obscure because she was never in the forefront.

Again, the opening this situation might present is not as great as one might initially suppose. All successful politicians will readily sacrifice their families to be accorded that magical "Mr. Mayor," "Senator," or "Mr. Representative."

One might possibly enlist the aid of a discarded spouse or child to uncover character weaknesses, but this is an often-contemplated, seldom-successful strategy. It was tried on President Reagan, for instance, with little notice or impact. Antagonistic members of the media often try to discredit sitting politicians by interviewing children who claim they did not vote for Mom or Dad. Impact of this ploy is minimal.

Politicians' lives are tied to finely tuned, detailed schedules. This fact more than many leads to openings that can be exploited by common people, especially if the politician's home state is distant from Washington, D.C. Even local pols run around in a frenzy trying to comply with the wishes of their scheduling secretary. Mayors, councilmen, commissioners, and such really do lead complex lives in terms of moving here and there to various meetings.

Some may disagree, but politicians are seldom, if ever successful, wise people. Test this theory by evaluating ones you know personally who have independently, without inheritance or chicanery, made even a reasonably decent living out in the real world. Obviously, few know anything about even simple concepts such as the law of supply and demand.

If there is one trait that characterizes a successful politician, it involves being extremely good with names. This class of people is accomplished at remembering people's names or has aides or spouses who can perform such work. In their offices, they keep extensive files on the rich and famous from within their districts along with issues of concern. Political monkey wrenchers should never assume that their politician does not know them on sight and could not quickly access information regarding children and spouse.

Whether politicians are leaders or are simply running hard to stay out in front of the howling mob is a good question. They poll a great deal attempting to stay ahead of issues of vital interest to their constituents. Protest all they want, but most are populists. "Let's take a poll to find out what the people want, and that is what I am in favor of," they usually say to their aides.

During the 16th and 17th centuries, horse-drawn coaches transporting people and goods rumbled along primitive roads. Coach dogs often ran along with these. Their job was to bark as the coach approached decision points. Some learned the way, but usually they ran behind the coach till it approached a fork in the road or a stop. Near the fork they ran on ahead, barking up both roads till the driver went down the correct fork. Then they followed till the next fork in the road.

Politicians today, in the quiet of their inner sanctums, refer to themselves as coach dogs. They try to bark up the correct trail as well as lead, but often they cannot do so successfully. Like coach dogs of yore, they try to give the impression that they know where the coach is headed, but in real life this is seldom true.

Politicians vote for or against legislation based on its falling in three broad classifications.

The first of these are moral-religious issues such as abortion, feminism, respect for the flag, or environmentalism. These are issues that impinge on that person's basic beliefs. It is seldom possible to induce a pol to vote in a manner that betrays these closely held beliefs. On the other hand, these issues seldom arise in their black and white form. Seasoned observers claim that at most this category of issues accounts for 5 percent of a pol's votes.

The next most important set of issues on which a pol votes comprises promises made during the most recent campaign. (Surprising as it sounds, politicians are actually embarrassed by having to vote contrary to promises made during the campaign. At best these issues make up another 30 percent of their votes.)

So, including moral issues, of the bills a pol will likely vote on, 35 percent relate to areas in which he cannot be lobbied.

Lastly, there is the great body of issues relating back to whom the pol is or was. These are issues decided by how the pol was raised, where he was raised, where his father worked, his family background, where he worked when going to school, which school he attended, his church background, and his experiences, such as automobile crashes and military service. Pols with parents who worked in the insurance business, for instance, are going to feel they know something about insurance issues. These are the areas in which the most successful lobbying takes place. It is also the area in which the greatest number of bills surface.

Little good is generally done attempting to influence politicians in the area of moral and campaign issues. Properly framed concepts, however, relating back to a pol's background and culture, can bear fruit. Always keep these concepts in mind when running political sting operations.

Politicians spend a great deal of time analyzing why people vote as they do. Voting patterns, they have discovered, are often complex. But they break out according to a few very basic rules that can be used by those fighting organized crime.

Citizens virtually always vote against a candidate rather than for one. It is our nature to determine whom we like least and then vote for the other person. Like the pols, we vote in a preconceived pattern based on past practice, upbringing, and beliefs. To the best of their ability, voters shut out contradictory information when deciding on candidates or issues. They don't choose to hear information or facts that contradict a preconceived notion. This explains why, when the whole world is moving away from political intervention and force, having proved it doesn't work, some people in the United States still think government officials can make better decisions than average citizens.

Democracies down through history have always degenerated into hordes of people attempting to vote themselves an advantage at the other guy's expense. At times, this often understandable greed can be used as a device or platform from which to attack politicians.

When contradictory or overtly selfish information becomes so intense in terms of weight or frequency that it can no longer be shut out or ignored, citizens will probably become confused, electing not to vote at all. Changing their minds becomes more odious than simply not voting. Experts claim that often this is one reason voter turnout is so light at many elections.

We also see why so many political events degenerate into

Pols will pull all sorts of silly stunts to get elected. Silly, unexpected stunts get them unelected.

mudslinging as pols attempt to reinforce the faithful believers, scare off the other side, and get citizens to oppose the other guy. Polls, in this context, are seen as having great value, not so much for identifying who is ahead, but as a means of identifying the issues and how to handle them. Undecideds, for instance, who are identified can be a gold mine if they can be moved into the positive category. Large numbers of undecideds are also seen as a threat if one has no workable plan to either move them or scare them into staying home.

Commonly, politicians spend very little time in their home states. George Bush may not even have actually been a resident of Texas. In several cases, western senators never visited their home states except to campaign. They attempted to ameliorate this behavior by opening several offices throughout their home states. Aides often appeared as surrogates for the candidates. When they finally did come back to campaign, local offices would take on the look of genuine, full-blown military campaigns. Dozens of aides ran in and out. Federal Express stopped with urgent parcels virtually daily. Giant wall charts and calendars looked much like military situation maps.

It is during these times, when people are thinking about issues and politicians and when expensive, tight schedules constrain the pols, that one can often intervene—with incredible results.

Other weak points exist. Some are fortuitous; some are characteristic of every campaign. In every case, we will try to cover only techniques that are common to pols or have been deployed successfully in the past.

It is with this very quick, very basic background in mind that we launch into real life, real meat issues of successfully fighting organized crime.

1 Little Things Mean a Lot

Politicians who, in the course of their campaigns, often appear on TV and at public gatherings tend to be a fastidious lot. They become very paranoid when their "dress for success" image is breached in any regard.

A wannabe pol running for national office placed his shoes outside his hotel room door as directed. A notice in his room indicated that a night valet would polish them while he slept.

We do not know if both shoes were ever polished. One was carried off and may still be in the hand of a political sting artist. They were $165 Ballys. Much to his horror, the guy was forced to show up at several early morning breakfasts wearing a pair of hotel slippers. They definitely did not match his slick, well-turned-out dark-suit-and-light-tie image.

Few people would actually have noticed, but the situation was exacerbated by the fact that our hero had to appear on a TV sitdown talk show, where he was forced to admit the very first thing that not everybody in town loved him. Instead of talking about issues, he was forced to talk first about shoes and petty theft.

It was not till an aide ran down to a local men's store at

10:00 A.M. when it first opened that things returned to normal. In the process, a precious $120 was spent—and, of course, the pol was thrown completely off stride.

Not a serious situation, most normal people suggest, but in this case it was considered to be serious enough to warrant a special staff meeting. A local field man, who was summarily fired over the event, still recalls the meeting, even though several years have intervened. He had nothing to do with the theft of one shoe, but an arrogant politician was adamant that someone should pay the price for so dastardly an act.

TAMPERING WITH TIGHT SCHEDULES

Sitting incumbents at higher levels usually have too much government-provided protection to make this sting work, but reportedly a team of monkey wrenchers attempted to stay ahead of the Dukakis presidential campaign, canceling his motel room, airline reservations, car rentals, and at times even his regularly scheduled political meetings.

Anonymous calls to local Democratic headquarters reportedly canceled appearances while setting up others in entirely unrelated or unsuspected locations. It was not uncommon for spurious reservations to be made for political gatherings in distant cities. Eventually a virtual torrent of bills, including overdue notices for motels, cars, and meeting room rentals, came flooding into campaign headquarters. Just getting these bills separated from legitimate ones became a major headache for an expensive staff worker.

These sorts of tricks don't always work, but at times Mr. Dukakis' schedule, for instance, became so snarled it seemed hopeless. Politicians always run on very complex, often intricate schedules, which explains why several senators wanted to dismantle United Airlines and sell it to Eskimos a few years back. In this case, United missed some flights, causing the pols a four-hour delay returning to Washington, D.C., for hearings.

When calling around to throw a monkey wrench in

Small rallies can be turned to the monkey wrencher's advantage.

appearances, speeches, motel reservations, airplane reservations, and other scheduled commitments, move them around rather than canceling. Change airplane reservations so that the guy misses flights on fly-or-die tickets, move coffees and motel rooms up, and schedule flights to places to which it is senseless to travel. If you can get credit card numbers, they can be used to rack up all kinds of charges for car rentals and tickets. Carefully plan so that no one turns up for scheduled meetings and that motels, tickets, and cars are reserved substantially before the group can arrive. This again generates generous overcharges that are a real financial blow to the campaign.

The rule of thumb for meetings is to cancel those with difficult, busy people, move those with small groups that won't be verified, and move or cancel only parts of large meetings. For instance, it probably wouldn't be effective to cancel a big dinner, but one can change the menus from steak to spaghetti, move the flowers to a day earlier, and book the banquet room for the A.M. rather than the P.M.

Pols try to organize large groups who wish to beat up on small groups. Using appropriate techniques, one can spoil their domestic lives, schedules, political plans, social lives, and finances.

Those who become familiar with campaign offices learn locations of light switches, door locks, telephone switch boxes, fuse boxes, water connections, sewers, burglar alarms, and all sorts of other good stuff. At a minimum, one could snip 2 inches out of the office telephone cable on the morning of an especially eventful day. Important conferences, fax transmissions, and other events could be disrupted by cutting power at the main meter, forcing the staff to call costly electricians and utility people. Usually something this overtly destructive should be done only after one is no longer volunteering.

As a general working rule, politicians running for most state or national offices will establish one or several local offices. Mayors and commissioners may very well run their campaigns out of their homes or their party headquarters. (Incumbent pols are supposedly not permitted to run campaigns out of their official offices. This prohibition is frequently violated but is of little concern to just about anyone. Most citizens just assume politicians are using public money to run their campaigns.) Call up the phone company and request that they disconnect the phones of those running campaigns from their homes. One could also go to the post office and forward all mail elsewhere (more on this area later). Call the power company and cancel their power or, better yet, steal the campaign headquarters power meter some dark night. One activist rigged an office sink so that it ran over, flooding the place.

Again, these are not particularly sophisticated devices, but when they disrupt the thief's schedule, they are laudatory.

POLITICAL ESPIONAGE

Setting up a successful political sting operation always requires that one initially become knowledgeable regarding the political campaign. This is sometimes quite difficult—especially at higher levels—and in other cases surprisingly easy. The best plan is probably to become associated with the campaign, either as an interested citizen or perhaps even as a volunteer. Just hanging around campaign headquarters a few days will uncover numerous opportunities.

Volunteers distribute literature, play the role of a warm body at news conferences, work on phone banks, address envelopes, drive cars, deliver materials, and organize coffees as well as many other equally fortuitous events. Obviously, if one wishes to run a political sting to influence a campaign adversely, his first duty will be (while doing little or no work) to quietly and unobtrusively collect as much literature and information about workings of the staff and campaign strategy as possible, not to mention working data about the staff, including names, addresses, and background data.

On knowing names of scheduling secretaries, field workers, supporters, and local organizers, one can go to work calling around in these people's names charging everything under the sun. One operator in Illinois secured the telephone

A union political beer bust in progress. An ideal time and place to do a bit of unseen reorganizing.

credit card number for the campaign. Instead of surreptitiously using the card to hype their phone bill $40 or $50 a month, he called Hong Kong, Turkey, and his girlfriend in England twice a day. A few extra dollars on the bill would have created strain without investigation, but almost $2,000 in weird expenses caused a great reaction.

The guy was caught as a result of an investigation into the called parties. He ended up paying a huge fine and lost his chance to deal with the thief effectively. Use caution and common sense when using purloined information.

GRASS ROOTS SABOTAGE

Politicians commonly engage in what is actually a reverse form of industrial espionage. They send their workers and volunteers to local churches, environmental groups, League of Women Voters forums, women's centers, neighborhood groups, unions, and any other local groups they can think of.

Fervor and actual physical attendance cycles with the campaign on a two- or six-year basis.

Volunteers and workers are supposed to leave a favorable impression with the group, steer its agenda in favor of the pol, and report back any important information. Opportunities for monkey wrenching here are obvious. One "volunteer" quietly let drop to a hard-core environmental group the fact that the pol was so desperate for campaign funds that he cut and sold the trees on his land. Another hinted to a women's group that the pol was a sucker for any lady with a truly magnificent chest. Subtlety counts heavily here, but this is exactly how political negativism gets started.

As mentioned, just a small, relatively insignificant comment can scare away supporters. Get enough of them out and enough people will be scared off.

UNCOVERING FINANCIAL INDISCRETIONS

Personal data on the pol can sometimes be uncovered by simply calling the campaign office and by obtaining a copy of his license.

"Hello, this is Mr. Smith calling from the FBI in Nashville," a typical pretext might run. "Is this the campaign headquarters for Sam Sleaze? We have been alerted that the vice president is considering making a trip out in support of your man. Could we please have the Social Security number of the candidate and two aides who might appear with him on the podium?" For years a friend of mine listed Richard Nixon's Social Security number on his bank CDs. All earnings were credited to Nixon's account by tax computers. Another fellow listed a pol's Social Security number every time he filled out insurance forms, accident reports, or official documents. Dozens of credit card applications he has made using pols' numbers are still floating around years after the targeted pols have retired.

It is relatively easy to go to a local credit bureau to get current information on a candidate, including Social Security numbers. Explain that as a small merchant you are concerned about requests by the campaign for credit. If they will only sell header information, that does not include actual credit data, take that. One can learn Social Security information, home address, wife and children's names, past residences, and employment history from this. A record of one's inquiry goes into the pol's credit record whenever the report is sold (not a good situation, but unless the pol's world really comes unhinged, he is not likely to think to check his credit file).

But best to start by popping a quick call to the state capitol. One can also secure fairly complete personal data on all state and national candidates through their sunshine reports and election petitions filed with the secretary of state. Secretary of state files are public records. One must pay anywhere from $3 to $15 for a credit report (depending on the credit bureau and what state the person requesting the report resides in), while secretary of state filings are charged by the sheet for copy expense. Sunshine reports list all contributions and expenses relative to a political campaign filed on a regular schedule with the secretary of state. Frequency of filing is set by state and federal law. Local candidates file with the county clerk. In many cases, minor local candidates such as mayor and councilman are exempt from filing financial data. Generally the media get more exercised because the pols don't have to file than because of what is included in the report.

Keep in mind that no piece of information is too trivial to be of value, provided that one is clever enough to twist it against the pol. For instance, many business people donate to opposing candidates in some form or another so they'll be assured favors no matter who wins. Even a hint that this game has been uncovered will dry up donations. One activist discovered that a local businessman had donated local office space to a pol. The businessman confirmed this state of affairs when contacted by the sting artist. However, when the sting artist cross-checked this information, he discovered that no listing for a donation of office space was included on the candidate's sunshine report. As in most states, laws

18

required this listing, which was actually deleted because the businessman wanted to remain anonymous.

Reporters at three of the state's larger newspapers and TV stations responded to this information only very lethargically. Generally, the media will not cover minor infractions, especially on the part of more liberal, interventionist-type candidates. However if, by some means or another, one subtly leads reporters to believe another TV station or newspaper might cover a story that they are overlooking, he may still succeed in pushing the piece into public view.

SIGNS OF TROUBLE

During the heat of an especially heavy campaign, political signs sprout up worse than mushrooms. At least mushrooms only grow where it is warm and damp. Some street corners support literally hundreds of pictures of smiling thieves. Most of us have probably thought about taking a day or two off work to go around the district collecting all those miserable symbols of tyranny and putting them into a great pile that could be torched.

A wire service story documented the fact that a man in Caldwell, Idaho, actually did go around collecting campaign signs. But rather than roasting wienies over them, he took only sound, usable plywood types, which he deployed as siding on his big double car garage and as subflooring in his new house.

High prices have forced some pols to use heavy cardboard, but wherever wind and rain might spoil paper, plywood is the medium of choice. Most pols want their "Vote for Me" signs to last at least as long as their promises.

These heavier plywood signs cost many dollars each, the local papers wailed, and this cruel, selfish prankster deprived worthy candidates of the opportunity to display their wares. If you believed the papers, democracy was threatened because this clever fellow found an inexpensive method of siding his garage. He placed all the faces inside, painting over the sign

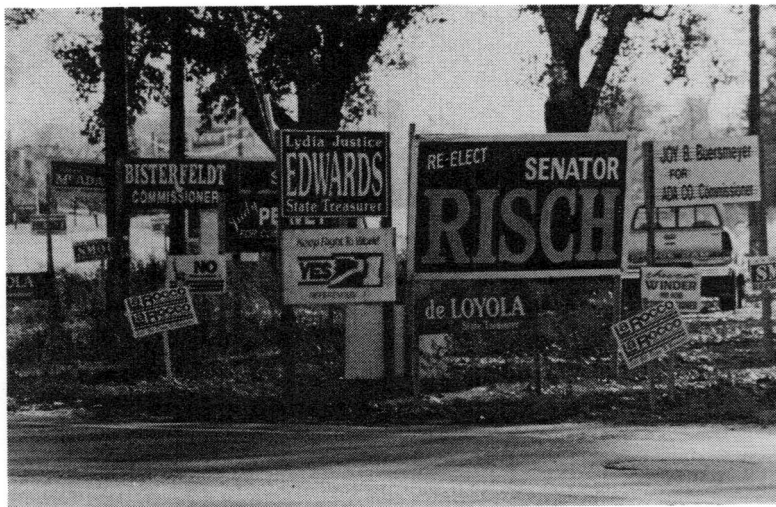

We are inundated by visual sound bites having no substance or purpose other than to get our vote.

backs outside. It was really weird to go inside the guy's garage, the paper said.

Given prices of building materials these days, the fellow traded a few hours of labor for something of great material benefit. Average citizens don't usually have an opportunity to do this at a pol's expense, but they should always be alert to the opportunity.

Most pols use literally hundreds of 4- x 8 1/2-inch-thick sheets of plywood for campaign signs. At current rates, these will run at least $10 each, not to mention cost of painting and stenciling on the message. In some classic cases, a pol running for office in a hot race will assume that he simply must keep a sign up at several key places around the district. (Allowing a blank at an especially busy intersection would be an admission that the opponent has more strength.) Thus, as fast as the signs are hauled away, the pol's staff will replace them. Smart monkey wrenchers remove the signs as quickly as possible. Really intelligent ones find productive uses for them.

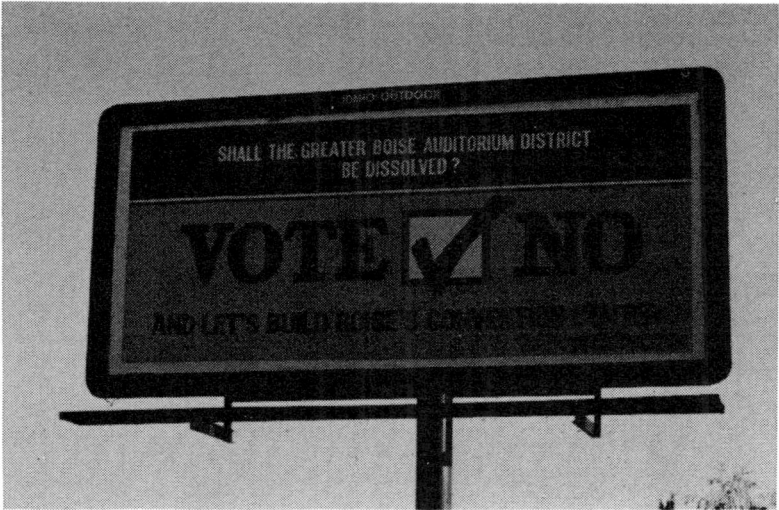

The process gets very convoluted, which presents ample opportunity for good monkey wrenchers to spread confusion. This billboard asks citizens to vote "no" to say "yes" . . .

If memory serves me, the hapless fellow in Caldwell, Idaho, was prosecuted for larceny. In many places, pols secure permission before posting signs. Most private property owners then assume some liability to see that the signs are not molested. Peculiar, since few pols these days have any concept of the very private property rights on which they rely in these cases.

At times one can locate a contract crew erecting the signs. These people will be doing the job simply as part of their work. One can often secure good information from these laborers, including numbers of signs to be erected, their intended locations, and even some idea of their cost.

Often private supporters call the pol asking that a sign be erected on their property. There is no pattern to this. It's just a matter of someone wanting a favor after the pol is in office.

Political monkey wrenchers have defaced these signs by drawing beards or spray painting obscenities on them, but the general consensus is that defacing, unless it is very clever, only draws attention to the pol and may even garner some sympathy for him. Yet very clever machine-printed paste-overs that change the entire meaning have been effective. "Senator Stump Wins for State" changed to "Wins for Self" is one example. One should always be alert for the opportunity to create a clever overlay. A pol put out hundreds of signs saying, "He's One of Us." A monkey wrencher overlaid nice painted strips so the sign read, "He's One of Them."

One man picked up an opposing pol's signs, cut the pictures from them, and glued them on the targeted pol's signs in place of his picture. It was a good hit, but one that would be unlikely given the need for two head shots that could be transposed.

Much ado was made about the fact that a hard-core environmentalist-type pol maliciously and destructively nailed his signs to some very nice trees. A good example of thinking one's way into a sting in a fashion that produces the greatest amount of grief for the greatest number of pols.

HITTING 'EM WHERE IT HURTS

Whether by specific design by the placing of soap in her milkshake (as we thought at the time) or as a result of other, more sophisticated sabotage, a candidate's wife got a serious case of diarrhea. It occurred at the exact time when she was to make a number of very public personal appearances in support of her candidate husband. The lady in this case was already reluctant to involve herself in all of this public hoopla.

As it transpired, her social embarrassment after riding in a small private aircraft and appearing at several gatherings was sufficiently severe that she made her candidate husband's life absolutely miserable for several weeks. She didn't like being out on display and she let her husband know it every chance she got.

It was a far easier and better sting than if someone would have dosed his milkshake. Effective monkey wrenchers keep the little things like this in mind.

2 Sleuthing in the Electronic Age

TAPPING INTO A WEALTH OF INFORMATION

Virtually all candidates campaigning for public office above the level of cemetery district or local dog catcher are paranoid regarding phone taps. This paranoia is perhaps well-founded. People running for public office spend a huge amount of time on the phone. Campaign headquarters are usually low-rent, temporary offices where telephone lines and junction boxes are accessed easily, and information commonly passed on phone lines could easily devastate a candidate if it were to fall into the wrong hands.

Large, well-financed campaigns for senator or representative are the exception, but generally little can be done within the targeted political group to counter or abate phone-tapping activities. The temptations to tap are great, the rewards of knowing campaign strategy and plans are tremendous, and physical features of the typical political office arrangement make it simple even for amateurs. In addition, there are usually very few people in and around a campaign qualified to uncover such activities.

Political handlers often bring in outside experts to check phone lines, but these are costly people who accomplish the ancillary goal of wasting campaign funds.

Phones are tapped by accessing phone wires within the building or phone junction box or, in many cases, by simply splicing into bare phone wires wherever one can find them. In many cases, there are dozens of pairs of wires leading into a pol's office. One must patiently listen and experiment till the correct, most profitable pair is located. Experts can quickly, easily discover these simple taps using visual or electronic devices. After one establishes a pattern of destructive use of phone information, it's safe to assume the tap will be found in a matter of days.

Transmitting intercepted phone conversations to those working on a political sting operation is done using FM radio transmitters, or, in the case of operators who can locate a listening post sufficiently close to their target, simple copper wires. FM transmitters are very low-power affairs set intricately on a narrow radio band snuggled in against a major commercial broadcaster. As a result, they are tough to locate with an FM receiver, and transmission distance is short—usually only 300 to 500 yards. If one can listen from an adjoining office without being observed, hard wire to this location is most desirable. Reception is clearer and accidental discovery is unlikely. But, if one cannot place a listening post relatively close to the pol's office, wires are not an option. For instance, we tapped the phones on the 13th floor of an office building where wires were impossible but FM radio transmissions worked nicely because of the altitude.

Rank amateurs can purchase phone tapping equipment from advertisers in Shotgun News. One can practice at home on his own phones till he gets the modest amount of skills required down. Costs for taps run between $15 and $200 or more per device. Personal experience suggests that lower-end—but not the cheapest—taps work sufficiently well.

A private contract telephone repairman living in New York claims that whenever he requires a tap he simply goes into a major apartment complex on a mission of discovery. At the complex' main switch panel, he claims he can usually find an abandoned tap of sufficient quality to do the work at hand. Even relatively expensive taps are so reasonably priced these days that it seldom pays to retrieve them after their work is completed. Ownership of taps is legal in the United States. Deployment, even against pols, is not. The guy says people in the complex had their phones tapped, and then when the listeners got the information they required, they simply abandoned the taps.

Taps operate either on batteries (that often must be replaced at great inconvenience) and/or power that comes directly from the phone system. Battery-powered taps are much tougher to locate by electronic means, but in most political situations this is of no consequence. If one must sneak into the premises at great risk, it will obviously be impractical to replace batteries every few days.

In the movies, phone tappers are traditionally characterized as sitting by a bare table, earphones in place, patiently listening to all line conversation in real time. It probably has never worked that way. Certainly it doesn't today. Wire tappers also invest in extremely long-play, voice-activated tape recorders that record and store all phone conversations so that one can listen to all at once, replaying them again and again as necessary.

Listening to phone taps is generally dreary, drab, monotonous work. Incredible amounts of trivia passes over the lines. Yet, now and then, one can pick out a major piece of news that has immediate importance. Poll results, speaking schedules, motel reservations, or spousal concerns have incredible value for monkey wrenchers.

Careful, patient phone tappers learn advertising schedules, budgets, names of supporters, travel plans, names of campaign workers, who is coming up with the best new ideas, and which angles and issues are giving the campaign strategists the worst scare. It takes some creativity to figure out how to use all of this material. If all else fails, send anonymous notes to opposing pols and the media regarding secret inner workings of the pol's office.

Initially, one might suppose it would be best to tap all of the pols, trading all their information around the industry. In reality, it is best to sting the incumbent hard, leaving ineffective neophytes alone and waiting until after they are in office to start the process of making life miserable for them.

An extremely bitchy wife with her broom on high prow forced her candidate husband to abandon the campaign mid-stream to take her on a four-day extended weekend vacation at a time when every minute was critical. Political moles found out about the wifely breach and the four-day hiatus. They passed the information to rivals, who planned fresh initiatives at a time when the incumbent could not respond. By the time the fellow returned and was out campaigning again, many charges had been laid to his account which he never overcame.

In another case, a mole placed a recorder on a tap set up in an old packing crate lying out in plain sight in a filthy, much-traveled public alley. Each night he crept in to remove the tape, which he played at home at his leisure. A great deal of what he heard was pap, except for a couple of conversations documenting the fact that several campaign workers were actually government employees who were supposed to be gainfully employed in other places as agency bureaucrats.

He managed to secure the bureaucrats' Social Security numbers and their government employee numbers. The pol's plan was supposedly to provide medical insurance for the workers, who intended to go on staff after he was elected. This information in itself was very damaging, but what the operator really wanted and never got via the tap was the pol's Social Security number.

Increasingly, computer data is passed between field workers and headquarters regarding schedules, issues, finances, strategies, plans, and answers to newly surfacing concerns. This information can be intercepted and used, but doing so usually requires the services of a computer techie. Simple

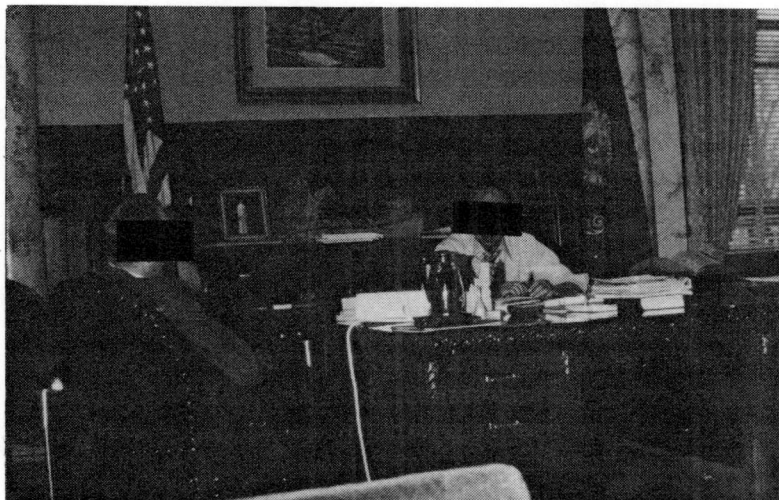

State governors have malicious powers. But they are fixed in place, where they become easy targets for monkey wrenchers.

taps can be deployed by motivated, bold amateurs, but collecting computer and fax data via surreptitious entry is a different ball game.

In some cases, phone tap information such as poll results, new issues that will be stressed, and major new endorsements are not easily, anonymously monkey-wrenched. In this case, one must decide if he is best served giving up his anonymity, selling or giving the data to a rival or sitting on the information till an appropriate opening occurs.

Those who provide excellent intelligence to rivals will gain a reputation for this good data. Later, toward the end of the campaign, one can provide totally fabricated, stupid data, making the recipients look like fools. This is a one-shot deal which, if not done correctly, will completely blow a sting artist's cover as well as flagging his intentions. Remember that in all cases the goal is to create confusion by working anonymously. If this isn't possible, settle for simply causing confusion.

BUGGING THEM

Phone taps are relatively easy and inexpensive for amateurs to deploy. Bugs, by contrast, are hidden, minute microphones set in places from which one wishes to monitor conversation. Bugs are usually more difficult to install and maintain.

Whereas phone taps pick up tons of extraneous garbage, room bugs multiply that factor by at least 10. Not only does it take much longer to sift through recordings from bugs, but in most cases they are tougher to install correctly.

Some bugs operate on 110-volt power secretly taken from wall sockets, but most operate on batteries that must be replaced periodically. The premises must be entered initially to place the bug and then again every few weeks to replace batteries.

Placement of bugs is critical. Locate one near a neon light or air conditioner and you will get nothing but hum. Placed under tables, they are out of sight but often also out of hearing of key speakers. Nothing is so aggravating as having a bug in place in a room through which people are walking while talking. Seems like the good stuff is always said just as they walk out of range into the next room.

Information from room bugs is transmitted via small FM transmitters or hard wire. In either case, one must have a listening post complete with voice-activated long-play tape recorder. Like taps, small, sophisticated bugs are available from advertisers in electronics magazines and *Shotgun News*.

Those who wish to try a simple, inexpensive, reasonably effective room bug should consider a Radio Shack wireless room intercom. These units can be hooked to one of the office outlets inside campaign headquarters using light 24- or 28-gauge wires, and they broadcast continuous signals out over existing building utility wires. They do a pretty good job of broadcasting everything said in a room, especially if they are wired into a light or outlet box high in a room away from refrigerators and air conditioners.

Rather than spending $150 on a battery-driven FM transmitter-type bug and whatever on a receiver and tape recorder, consider using a Radio Shack wireless intercom. If entrance and placement of this device are successful, consider using a more sophisticated device.

DUMPSTER DIVING AS AN ALTERNATIVE

If you are not committed to using electronic means of information gathering, give serious thought to political Dumpster diving. Real nuggets of gold await those persistent and determined enough to sift through the campaign waste baskets. Increasingly campaign managers insist on the use of shredders, but good stuff has a way of slipping through the procedure into trash cans that are in turn dumped into Dumpsters. As late as the first Bush campaign a complete, intact strategy book found its way from the Dukakis Dumpster to the Bush campaign headquarters and out again to the Bush Dumpster.

Information can include credit card carbons, copies of expense account data, telephone records, call-back messages, restaurant receipts, and names of staffers, supporters, organizers, and new people supporting the campaign. There may even be copies of speeches, references to unlisted phone numbers and secret numbers in Washington, D.C., and notes on medications the pol must take. Get the name of the pol's doctor and you can, by some ruse or another, secure a copy of his medical data. In one case, operatives discovered where a campaign car that was to be used in a parade was garaged. The vehicle never made it to the parade.

In Detroit a sting artist offered $10 per bag for any paper that street people could salvage from campaign headquarters. Leads generated from this jumble gave a contender enough to throw an entrenched incumbent sufficiently off track that the voters unhired him.

3 Media

No matter where one comes down on the Clarence Thomas affair, this incident does provide evidence that the American newspaper and television media have different sets of standards for liberals and conservatives. This is no problem for political sting artists as long as they understand there are different ground rules. Our media, for instance, won't pay much attention to liberal sexual peccadilloes but will come down hard on the same person who runs a profitable business deal.

No matter what they say in public, all pols privately hate newspaper, TV, and even radio people with an absolute passion. The real trick for any of them is to keep this hatred controlled and under cover. I have known numerous pols for all of whom this has been true. They force themselves to be nice and to get along, but often this is only a very superficial act.

A West Coast manipulator used both his real name and an alias to write to his U.S. representative asking the pol to support opposite sides of the same issue. Both letters were returned to the same address, but the pol's staff in D.C. didn't catch it. In his responses to both letters, the congressman assured the writer that he supported his position and had voted accordingly, meaning, in summary, that he voted both yes and no on a particularly hot issue. Because of procedural rules in state and national legislatures, this is actually possible. He changed his yes vote to a no on roll call after he saw that there were enough votes to pass the bill. Then he asked for a vote of reconsideration, which failed. All this allowed him to validly claim he voted both yes and no on the same bill. Other, more sophisticated procedures are available, but this relatively simple and common one is the one he used. What got the pol in trouble were his letters of about the same date taking opposing sides on the issue.

Newspapers in the area refused to run the two letters side by side, even as paid advertisements. Eventually, the sting artist found a small weekly paper in his district that agreed to run the two letters with his brief comments as a paid ad. After that, several other papers and the local TV station picked up on the concept.

Instead of concentrating on the duplicity of the pol, the media severely chastised the sting artist for using trickery when obtaining the two opposing letters. He was also accused of being devious and unfairly attacking a hard-working public servant. Assuredly attendants in Hitler's death camps were hard working, but we seldom consider this to be laudable. At any rate, the sting should have had more impact but failed to catch the public's attention. That is a risk we take in this business.

Placing the ad cost a reasonable amount of money, which my friend split among associates who formed a small ad hoc committee to handle the affair. In spite of the committee, the incident managed to expose him as a political monkey wrencher, precluding him from gathering additional information around the campaign. Now, rather than placing ads, he has developed a computerized list of activist types in his district to whom he plans to mail copies of any contradictory statements.

On several occasions, voters and reporters have asked the pol about his contradictory stands, often in public forum. Rather than answering the question, the pol launches into a personal attack on the fellow who received the letters. Unfortunately, at this writing, the pol still holds his office.

In most cases, however, this kind of exposure is a problem. Politicians who know that someone is actively trying to sabotage their efforts tend to add caution.

The clever sting artist finally moved to another congressional district, where he often writes his congressman urging contradictory positions. Eventually, he believes, he will get another bingo, starting the process anew.

Back a few years, before computer scanners made it ridiculously easy, a select few political sting artists worked actively in the subtle art of creating and distributing phony press releases. Usually members of the pol's reelection committee would create these to sabotage the opposition. At times they were ham-handed obvious because the content was so outrageous. Other times they were sufficiently subtle that they actually found their way into the media.

Currently there are no proven cases of freelancers having produced bogus news releases that actually made the news. But one can only assume fed-up citizens will soon deploy them on a personal level.

Start by securing a copy of the pol's campaign stationery. Calling party headquarters or writing a letter will usually generate a response. Mass mailings sent out by the pol often will include a sheet of stationery. The fact that the sheet contains a great deal of other copy makes no difference given modern computer scanners. If nothing is available, create something from scratch using a bumper sticker or whatever as a scanner pattern. This is all we used in years past, often with good effect.

As a custom of the trade, new release forms include the logo at the top and the name and telephone number of a campaign contact person at the right top of the page. Under the name, place both a daytime phone number and a home phone number. The best results are probably obtained by faking this name and number. If reporters call for clarification, they will get a wrong number.

In many cases, rather than looking up the correct number,

they will go ahead and run the story. Reporters are very harried. Once the decision has been made to run the piece, they are like the homebound draft horse. Media that are geographically or socially farther from the campaign are more gullible in this regard. Tiny weeklies that are often left off of everyone's mailing list tend to run without checking.

Type the date of release to the left above the body of the article. Place the words "FOR IMMEDIATE RELEASE" just below that. On the top right-hand side of the page, type the name of a contact person and below that a phone number.

Copy for the text should read exactly like a typical newspaper story. In this instance, writing a story is not difficult once one has thought of a clever angle to use. As in all newspaper stories, start with a city name and state, leading into a clever one-sentence hook that serves to draw readers into the piece.

A typical but entirely fictitious humorous lead might read:

(San Lucas, TX)—Senator Snort, speaking before a large group of taxidermists today, said that his opponent can stuff it.

Don't use the above example; it has already been tried. Fake news releases must be extremely subtle to work. While it would be fun to belittle the pol in a release, it is seldom possible. The goal in these cases is not to give reporters a good laugh but to cast doubt regarding the guy's consistency, integrity, and intelligence without being overt.

Sting experts have had excellent results explaining in a bogus news release why a pol refused to attend a League of Women Voters forum when, in fact, that pol actually attended and spoke. Another device is to subtly claim in the phony news release from the pol that he is having staff problems, that environmentalists are actually members of a left wing religious group, that churches should be taxed, or that the new recycling center should be sold to private business.

Keep in mind that political issues cycle dramatically and that in addressing these issues in the fake news release, one must be subtle and timely. Carefully evaluate current issues and get out a phony news release that makes the pol look stupid, uninformed, out of step, prejudiced, or all of the above.

Lists of radio, TV, and newspapers within a congressional district can be obtained from a local chamber of commerce. As a general rule, even very well done, clever fake news releases put together on good copies of the candidate's stationery counterfeited with a computer and laser printer only work once or perhaps twice during a single campaign. Yet they are effective if one wishes to harass a sitting pol safe back in his D.C. office, basically unaware of what is happening at the local level.

Other complimentary sting techniques are available to motivated citizens. The fake radio actuality is a dynamite device because industry people assume no citizen knows how actualities work. They genuinely believe that this device could not be subverted.

Actualities are brief, usually live sound bites recorded from recent speeches made by the candidate which are transmitted to various radio stations by campaign headquarters.

The campaign press director will make recordings of a speech and pull out two or three punchy sentences that are then recorded onto a master tape. All actualities are very short. Radio news people never, never use more than a few words from a candidate. Offering more is a sure sign all is not kosher.

Before the brief statement, which is generally so short just about anyone can fake it, record in the time, day, and date as well as the name of the group to which the candidate was speaking. These are played over the phone for radio station news directors.

Conditions change region to region, but generally radio stations are delighted to receive short, timely news clips. Call the radio station news director claiming that you have a 12-second actuality from Senator Snort (or whoever). Cut the earphone from the recorder's external microphone and solder in two small alligator clips, one to each wire. Plug this connection into the tape machine's external microphone port. After the radio station news director says "OK," unscrew the speaker portion of the phone handset and connect the alligator clamps to the two internal wires in the phone.

The tape player will send the recording to the radio news director over the phone line. He will record the piece on his end. Line distortion is so bad that the scam almost always works. No one can tell it isn't the pol speaking.

Disconnect the alligator clips and reassemble the phone. Check with the news director to be sure he got the actuality. Radio's great selling feature is timeliness and speed. Often these actualities find their way into the very next news broadcast. They will only be used three or four times at the most.

As mentioned, tape recording and telephone interference obscure the candidate's voice a bit. Virtually anyone who practices can fool radio news directors. Call in the name of a fictitious political news director. If radio people ask about the regular news director, tell them you are "helping out as a volunteer today."

Wild and crazy stuff such as claiming the candidate is considering closing a local military base, favors firing a local EPA administrator, or wants to establish a regional dump or perhaps a special detention camp for AIDS patients, and any other strange statements work well. These stings work because radio stations do not expect them since few people know how to put together actualities and because smaller radio stations are so anxious for current live news.

It hasn't been done yet that I know of, but someday someone will get a totally off-the-wall comment supposedly made by a pol onto local radio and tie it to a news release that he has made up and sent to the papers. The combination will put the pol in the position of declaring war on England, giving Alaska back to the Russians, or memorializing Cuba for its great economic progress. Skillfully coordinated at the end of a campaign, this device could actually sink a candidate.

Perhaps it is an apocryphal tale told of President Franklin Roosevelt, who used a radio chat format to campaign.

Reportedly Roosevelt was outdone by a rival pol who bought a block of time on network news immediately following the president. Roosevelt was denied the chance to have the last word in this instance. But Roosevelt, so the story goes, simply penciled out a few lines from his speech, allowing the radio to go silent for a few minutes before his opponent started his speech. Naturally, the story goes, most Americans turned their radios off for the night and the rival pol was heard by only a few people.

It is doubtful whether the average political monkey wrencher could ever take advantage of this type of sting. But one could call all of the radio and TV stations and newspapers in the district, canceling all of the candidate's paid advertisements. Claim you are the pol's media purchasing director and that severe money problems have created the need to call in all paid advertising.

If the business manager says, "We don't have any paid media booked with your office," tell him, "We have you down for a $3,000 budget—you are _____ (use the name of that outfit's principal rival), aren't you?" Use this device late in the campaign, as it will guarantee that outfit will never voluntarily say another nice thing about the candidate.

Political ads must be prepared well ahead of the time they are scheduled to run. Don't say how or why, but tell the advertising manager that there is no money to cover checks already written for advertisements. Don't try this ploy with billboard people. Their space is booked and paid for as much as eight months ahead.

Arguments between campaign news directors and radio, TV, and newspapers are fairly common. They arise over tone, content, timing, and conclusions of news stories run by these media. Call claiming you are the pol's new media person and that your boss objects to a recent story. Argue some off-the-wall point that subtly changes the meaning and policy of the pol. Arguing that a liberal pol does not really support welfare or that children should be allowed to work at age 12 are some examples.

Usually news people will ask you to have the pol call back

personally. Tell the reporter you will have him do that but right now he is flying to Moscow to meet the new government, or whatever. Keep arguing with the reporter till things turn very sour.

Most of these devices work only once per campaign or term of office per pol. More may be possible if one is especially clever. Yet fake radio actualities have been done several times a year, especially when they are clever and subtle. Pols cannot hope to listen to every radio news program throughout their district. When they have been used, the pol first finds out about them when somebody asks a question about a foolish position they assume he had taken on an issue.

These stings require a bit of thought, creativity, and brass. Modern electronic equipment makes them easier. They will create controversy and confusion that will reverberate throughout the district.

4 Finding Others to Spend the Pol's Money

Politicians find that campaign funds are never sufficient to accomplish the goals they set. This is true even in supposedly safe districts where membership in the prevailing party or incumbency virtually guarantee a free ride. As a rule, pols spend a great deal of time and energy raising money. Any wastage of funds once in their hot, grubby hands is viewed as an extremely serious matter.

Two methods of effectively attacking a pol financially are available to the average concerned citizen. First, one can waste money by ordering unwanted, unneeded items in the pol's name, creating financial confusion within his organization. Citizens can also attack the pol's credibility in such a manner that political investors are scared away. To a great extent, using devices outlined in other chapters can and does have the effect of driving off contributors, especially if they are individuals and business people.

Political action committees (PACs), in contrast, cut their own private side deals with pols. These are tough to get between. Political contributions are, according to the pols, investments in good government. They are really socially acceptable bribes. But such philosophical stuff is beyond the scope of this book.

Fund wastage was perfected by a couple of little known political sting artists during the '70s. They came up with a program of charity, giving in the name of virtually all of the pols in their area. This device proved to be gifted in its inception.

They proceeded basically as follows. Absolutely every time a public charity solicited money, they called the phone bank or sent in a pledge card in the pol's name. Pledges they committed in the pol's name were healthy to fat. They were large enough to be believable and to catch people's eye, but not so large as to look phony. In this regard, careful planning was necessary.

Best impact occurred when the pledge was announced openly as it came in to phone banks, a central office, or whatever. Immediately after the pledge was acknowledged, another fellow called saying he was a political rival who was genuinely concerned about this particular cause. He was not interested in politics and, to show this to be true, was doubling his rival's pledge. His concern came from the heart and not out of expediency. It was so corny most people were turned off!

Later on in the event, they called again with marbles in their mouths, cotton in their noses, and handkerchiefs over the telephone, till they had virtually every pol in the area, from mayor to U.S. senator, pledged up to a maximum. Their efforts resulted in the drive going way over its goals.

Had people from any one of the pols' offices been listening, they could have stopped the sting. But, ironically, nobody from these offices was paying any attention to these boring fund drive programs. Later, when the pols found out about their obligations, it provided yet another round of embarrassment. It became even more grim when the fund raisers found out it was all a scam. They blamed the pols for not meeting their goals and for cheaply using the event for their own advancement.

All of this made glorious headlines in the local media off and on for several weeks. As it concluded, a few of the pols who had relatively large campaign funds were forced by public opinion to honor their pledges. Part of the sting hinged on the resultant media investigations into the money the pols intended to spend on campaigning and their speculating about putting a small part into a worthy cause. In a few cases the pols were forced to admit that they really didn't personally support AIDS research, contribution to the homeless, or whatever, in order to get out of their pledges. The sting provided a graphic demonstration to the public that some liberal candidates can be extremely liberal with other people's money but are grinchlike with their own funds.

One must be alert for fund-raising events in which this ploy is effective. They include telethons and benefits for public TV, hospitals, municipalities, schools, cancer, heart disease, AIDS, homelessness, and environmental causes, to name a few.

Another pol espoused an especially radical left wing group's agenda. An alert sting artist ordered several hundred of that group's expensive propaganda books through it's toll-free order line. The books were charged to the pol in the name of his office. The fellow ordering claimed the books were to be given away free throughout the pol's office.

Fortunately, the radical group got out a news release praising the pol for his gutsy stand on controversial social issues. All of the boxes of books arrived at the pol's office several weeks before the statement. His staff thought they were a gift, treating them rather cavalierly. By the time the bill arrived, it was too late to return them.

This imbroglio boiled beneath the surface for several months. Eventually, the pol authorized payment for the books rather than risking alienation of the group and its many members. The books were carefully chosen by the sting artist for having information of little social or scientific value.

As far as anyone knows, the volumes are still stored in the pol's garage. They definitely fulfilled their role of drawing away about $1,500 in precious funds. This strategy works best when the pol is sitting safely far away in his Washington, D.C., office and the volumes are delivered to his office within the state of residence.

If one cannot orchestrate a major purchase such as making a pledge or ordering a batch of expensive, arcane books, it is always possible to make up for quality with quantity. It was Joseph Stalin who, when told his T-54 battle tanks were of low quality, said, "There is a certain quality to large quantities."

In the name of the pol or one of his staff, order pizza, ice cream, flowers, Chinese food, singing telegrams, professional entertainers, gravel, fertilizer, tow trucks, a side of beef, jewelry, and other items from the TV shopper, bottled water, security guards, and any other goods or services one can imagine when thumbing through the yellow pages.

Don't forget to invite life insurance salesmen, real estate agents, and especially advertising agents to come down to the pol's local office to give their pitches. Call in the name of a fictitious office worker and actually make a specific appointment. Intimate that you have already decided to purchase their service and that all that you need is a contract to sign.

Try, when scrounging up appointments, to include as many gimmicky nail file and calendar type advertising sellers as humanly possible. These people are incredibly skilled and persistent, and often they will actually end up selling something useless to the pol's staff. Be sure to call every printer in the city, as these people profit big time from political campaigns and will climb over their dead mothers' bodies to be first in line to talk to the pol and his staff.

Many of these people, who show up in person, will not be able to get into the pockets of the pol, but they will get under the staff's skin. When they leave, they will have very negative feelings about the pol and his staff. In all cases, they will throw sand in a finely tuned machine.

Political staffs are normally very busy, very easily distracted organizations. They operate on the premise that "those who make the fewest errors last will win." Throw a glitch into their procedure and you have accomplished quite a lot more than wasting money.

One can spend money for the pol by going to coupon advertisers, sky writers, heating and cooling people, janitorial services, and casualty insurance agencies and signing expensive contracts for service. In places where they insist on payment up front, tell the sales agent that you will return with a check and walk out. Most will start their service at the same time they mail the bill to the pol's office address. All will call repeatedly, asking what happened to their deal made with your employee.

One will definitely want to sign up for every magazine subscription in the United States, every Florida land deal, every tombstone insurance program, and every midnight extermination service that can be found. Do all on behalf of one's beloved pol.

Look in the section titled "Relationships" in a reference book titled Writers' Market, which can be found at the local library in the reference section. Specific names, addresses, and even 800 numbers are listed for virtually all the magazines in the nation catering to perverted life-styles. One can easily, systematically order up subscriptions to these nefarious publications for the pol or his staff.

However, it is far more effective to determine the name of one of the staff and order a subscription in that name. Also, list the fact that this magazine is going to the senator's assistant at the pol's office. As a final measure, after using a real name with real political headquarters, have the magazine intentionally mis-sent to the real street address of a near neighbor who you suspect would be very offended upon learning that such smut circulates freely through the mail and is supposedly being received by people on the pol's staff.

Expert political handlers speculate that only three or four subscriptions that fall into the wrong hands in certain districts could actually influence an election or force an incumbent pol not to run for office again. Smaller, tightly knit, more conservative districts where the pol is running for mayor or commissioner are most vulnerable to this device.

All of these devices have a direct and, in most cases, financial and moral impact on a pol. But what to do if the bastard lied through his teeth, won the election, and now sits in the great capital of whoredom making decisions for you when one would never voluntarily even talk with the guy under normal circumstances?

A device exists that is very new to the trade but shows great promise. *Forbes* business magazine reports that this ploy is just starting to be used in earnest on individuals and that, at the time of this writing, no defense exists. In most cases, those hit by this sting were forced to hire lawyers and CPAs costing more than the amount they owed the Internal Revenue Service (IRS) as a result of the sting. The report emphasized the fact that once this device went into motion, *nobody* escaped.

Filing bogus Internal Revenue Service 1099 forms constitutes the core of this device. The IRS requires 1099 forms when a nonemployee taxpayer receives any money for any reason, including consulting services, royalties, contract work, rents, prizes, awards, and any nonemployee compensation. Companies or individuals must file these documents with the IRS indicating that they have paid whatever amount of money to a person, and normally they also send carbon copies to the recipient of the funds, who certainly already knows that he has been paid by the reporting concern.

The wonderful thing about 1099s is that the recipient does not know they are being filed unless he receives such a carbon copy, and the government always takes the filing at face value. Most experts believe that, as use of phony 1099s explodes, Congress will either lose many numbers because of charges of tax evasion, or they will be forced to change current rules and regulations. At present these forms constitute one of the biggest, baddest hits one can make on thieves in the United States.

When 1099s are used as part of a sting, the pol does not

9595 ☐ VOID ☐ CORRECTED

PAYER'S name, street address, city, state, and ZIP code		1 Rents $ 2 Royalties $ 3 Prizes, awards, etc. $	OMB No. 1545-0115 1993	Miscellaneous Income
PAYER'S Federal identification number	RECIPIENT'S identification number	4 Federal income tax withheld $	5 Fishing boat proceeds $	Copy A For Internal Revenue Service Center File with Form 1096. For Paperwork Reduction Act Notice and instructions for completing this form, see Instructions for Forms 1099, 1098, 5498, and W-2G.
RECIPIENT'S name		6 Medical and health care payments $	7 Nonemployee compensation $	
Street address (including apt. no.)		8 Substitute payments in lieu of dividends or interest $	9 Payer made direct sales of $5,000 or more of consumer products to a buyer (recipient) for resale ► ☐	
City, state, and ZIP code		10 Crop insurance proceeds $	11 State income tax withheld $	
Account number (optional)	2nd TIN Not. ☐	12 State/Payer's state number		

Form **1099-MISC** Cat. No. 14425J Department of the Treasury - Internal Revenue Service

Do NOT Cut or Separate Forms on This Page

9595 ☐ VOID ☐ CORRECTED

PAYER'S name, street address, city, state, and ZIP code		1 Rents $ 2 Royalties $ 3 Prizes, awards, etc. $	OMB No. 1545-0115 1993	Miscellaneous Income
PAYER'S Federal identification number	RECIPIENT'S identification number	4 Federal income tax withheld $	5 Fishing boat proceeds $	Copy A For Internal Revenue Service Center File with Form 1096. For Paperwork Reduction Act Notice and instructions for completing this form, see Instructions for Forms 1099, 1098, 5498, and W-2G.
RECIPIENT'S name		6 Medical and health care payments $	7 Nonemployee compensation $	
Street address (including apt. no.)		8 Substitute payments in lieu of dividends or interest $	9 Payer made direct sales of $5,000 or more of consumer products to a buyer (recipient) for resale ► ☐	
City, state, and ZIP code		10 Crop insurance proceeds $	11 State income tax withheld $	
Account number (optional)	2nd TIN Not. ☐	12 State/Payer's state number		

Form **1099-MISC** Cat. No. 14425J Department of the Treasury - Internal Revenue Service

Do NOT Cut or Separate Forms on This Page

9595 ☐ VOID ☐ CORRECTED

PAYER'S name, street address, city, state, and ZIP code		1 Rents $ 2 Royalties $ 3 Prizes, awards, etc. $	OMB No. 1545-0115 1993	Miscellaneous Income
PAYER'S Federal identification number	RECIPIENT'S identification number	4 Federal income tax withheld $	5 Fishing boat proceeds $	Copy A For Internal Revenue Service Center File with Form 1096. For Paperwork Reduction Act Notice and instructions for completing this form, see Instructions for Forms 1099, 1098, 5498, and W-2G.
RECIPIENT'S name		6 Medical and health care payments $	7 Nonemployee compensation $	
Street address (including apt. no.)		8 Substitute payments in lieu of dividends or interest $	9 Payer made direct sales of $5,000 or more of consumer products to a buyer (recipient) for resale ► ☐	
City, state, and ZIP code		10 Crop insurance proceeds $	11 State income tax withheld $	
Account number (optional)	2nd TIN Not. ☐	12 State/Payer's state number		

Form **1099-MISC** Cat. No. 14425J Department of the Treasury - Internal Revenue Service

The official IRS form 1099 can be used as the basis for an extremely hard-hitting sting.

know that funds have been credited to his tax account when he prepares his taxes. IRS computers have the amount of income claimed by various payers, which they match to the amount on the pol's tax return. When they

DO NOT STAPLE   6969

Form **1096**	Annual Summary and Transmittal of U.S. Information Returns	OMB No. 1545-0108
Department of the Treasury Internal Revenue Service		19**93**

FILER'S name

Street address (including room or suite number)

City, state, and ZIP code

If you are not using a preprinted label, enter in box 1 or 2 below the identification number you used as the filer on the information returns being transmitted. Do not fill in both boxes 1 and 2.	Name of person to contact if the IRS needs more information	For Official Use Only
	Telephone number ( )	

1 Employer identification number	2 Social security number	3 Total number of forms	4 Federal income tax withheld $	5 Total amount reported with this Form 1096 $

Check only one box below to indicate the type of form being transmitted.   If this is your FINAL return, check here . . . ▶ ☐

W-2G 32	1098 81	1099-A 80	1099-B 79	1099-DIV 91	1099-G 86	1099-INT 92	1099-MISC 95	1099-OID 96	1099-PATR 97	1099-R 98	1099-S 75	5498 28
☐	☐	☐	☐	☐	☐	☐	☐	☐	☐	☐	☐	☐

Please return this entire page to the Internal Revenue Service. Photocopies are NOT acceptable.

Under penalties of perjury, I declare that I have examined this return and accompanying documents, and, to the best of my knowledge and belief, they are true, correct, and complete.

Signature ▶ ....   Title ▶ ....   Date ▶ ....

Instructions

Purpose of Form.—Use this form to transmit paper Forms 1099, 1098, 5498, and W-2G to the Internal Revenue Service. DO NOT USE FORM 1096 TO TRANSMIT MAGNETIC MEDIA. See Form 4804, Transmittal of Information Returns Reported Magnetically/Electronically.

Use of Preprinted Label.—If you received a preprinted label from the IRS with Package 1099, place the label in the name and address area of this form inside the brackets. Make any necessary changes to your name and address on the label. However, do not use the label if the taxpayer identification number (TIN) shown is incorrect. **Do not prepare your own label. Use only the IRS-prepared label that came with your Package 1099.**

If you are not using a preprinted label, enter the filer's name, address (including room, suite, or other unit number), and TIN in the spaces provided on the form.

Filer.—The name, address, and TIN of the filer on this form must be the same as those you enter in the upper left area of Form 1099, 1098, 5498, or W-2G. A filer includes a payer, a recipient of mortgage interest payments (including points), a broker, a barter exchange, a person reporting real estate transactions, a trustee or issuer of an individual retirement arrangement (including an IRA or SEP), and a lender who acquires an interest in secured property or who has reason to know that the property has been abandoned.

Transmitting to the IRS.—Send the forms in a flat mailing (not folded). Group the forms by form number and transmit each group with a **separate** Form 1096. For example, if you must file both Forms 1098 and 1099-A, complete one Form 1096 to transmit your Forms 1098 and another Form 1096 to transmit your Forms 1099-A. You need not submit original and corrected returns separately.

Box 1 or 2.—Complete only if you are not using a preprinted IRS label. Individuals who are in a trade or business must enter their social security number in box 2; sole proprietors and all others must enter their employer identification number in box 1. However, sole proprietors who do not have an employer identification number must enter their social security number in box 2.

Box 3.—Enter the number of forms you are transmitting with this Form 1096. Do not include blank or voided forms or the Form 1096 in your total. Enter the number of correctly completed forms, not the number of pages, being transmitted. For example, if you send one page of three-to-a-page forms 1096 with a Form 1096 and you have correctly completed two Forms 5498 on that page, enter 2 in box 3 of Form 1096.

Box 4.—Enter the total Federal income tax withheld shown on the forms being transmitted with this Form 1096.

Box 5.—No entry is required if you are filing Form 1099-A or 1099-G. For all other forms, enter the total of the amounts from the specific boxes of the forms listed below:

Form W-2G	Box 1
Form 1098	Boxes 1 and 2
Form 1099-B	Boxes 2 and 3
Form 1099-DIV	Boxes 1a, 5, and 6
Form 1099-INT	Boxes 1 and 3
Form 1099-MISC	Boxes 1, 2, 3, 5, 6, 7, 8, and 10
Form 1099-OID	Boxes 1 and 2
Form 1099-PATR	Boxes 1, 2, 3, and 5
Form 1099-R	Box 1
Form 1099-S	Box 2
Form 5498	Boxes 1 and 2

For more information and the Paperwork Reduction Act Notice, see the Instructions for Forms 1099, 1098, 5498, and W-2G.   Form **1096** (1993)

Cat. No. 144000

IRS *form* 1096 *is used to transmit* IRS *form* 1099.

don't match, the IRS sends out a tax deficiency notice claiming added taxes, interest, and penalties due. As reported in the media, it takes a few years, but there is no way to get out of paying extra taxes based on the amount placed in the bogus 1099 form. Usually this is approximately one-third of the amount reported.

Political sting artists can get these blank documents from virtually any local CPA or tax attorney.

Some underground tax people claim that fake 1099s will work without the recipient's Social Security number if a full address is used. But most claim to be certain one must include the pol's Social Security number. Other than this, the form is extremely simple. These same experts suggest that rather than getting carried away listing hundreds of thousands in "extra" income, that more plausible amounts such as 30 to 40 grand per senator and representative in payment for speaking engagements be listed. Mayor and commissioner types can generally be impacted with as little as $10,000 to $12,000 of which one-third will show up as delinquent taxes. If more money seems to be appropriate, file two, three, or even four bogus 1099s, using different bogus companies for each.

There is a transmittal form that should go with the 1099s to the IRS. It is called a form 1096. One is supposed to list employee identification numbers on this form. Either make them up or lift them from legitimate tax papers from existing companies. Although most of this is untested, some experts recommend that real company names be used on both forms, even if employee identifications are fabricated.

Again, the IRS always assumes that these 1099s are accurate and legitimate and will aggressively pursue collection of taxes they think were illegally avoided as a result of nonreporting of these 1099s.

When several 1099s for lesser amounts are filed, they seem to require the pol to seek more extensive professional legal services. Reliable reports indicate that bogus 1099 increases of $13,000 to $20,000 result in $5,000 to $7,000 tax bills which have *never* been cleared for less than $8,000 to $10,000 each. This plus the publicity can be a real hit on a pol. For once the pol can be made to feel like the poor, suffering taxpayer out in the trenches.

One can only smile at the prospect of several of these fake 1099s being filed on every pol in the area, including mayors and members of fascist planning and zoning commissions. These misguided souls so intent on stealing property for their own use would find the price of crime to be pretty high. It would take time, but the procedure would ruin all of them, unless Congress were to change the laws.

The only tough part is doing it right and securing needed Social Security numbers. Do this by pretext, calling the pol's office and campaign headquarters or using information obtained from a credit report, driver's license, or papers filed with the secretary of state.

Using this simple expedient, it may be possible to break even people like the Kennedys. Filing phony 1099s will remain the atomic bomb of political activism, at least till this information is widely disseminated and laws are changed.

5 The Mailman Can Help

Absolutely all of what follows is true. Each device has been deployed successfully by various political sting activists—many on rival politicians' payrolls. Unfortunately, all range from being illegal to very illegal. For this reason, we must be somewhat obscure about who exactly deployed these devices and suggest that the material that follows is *for information and entertainment purposes only.*

A somewhat obscure candidate serving as senator of a smaller, insignificant state decided to test bigger and better waters by running in a U.S. presidential primary. (This in and of itself suggests that the arrogance factor for some of these people is tremendous.)

His initial budget was rather modest, but he tried to play the big time with slick brochures and postage-paid return envelopes—some of the first targeted direct mail advertising.

Reportedly, political sting artists sank the campaign shortly after its birth, in large part by wasting the fellow's money away before he could get rolling, including scaring off big-money donors who normally finance such things. One of their most successful money-wasting ploys was the diversion of funds into bogus business reply envelopes.

MAKING NEGATIVE DONATIONS

This is a somewhat expensive device, but it has the added advantage of its psychological impact and the fact that anyone using a prepaid business reply envelope (BRE) is vulnerable. In terms of total cost, the impact is modest, yet these costs come right off the top at a time when pols can least afford them. The psychological impact is tough for anyone outside of politics to envision. How some candidates face the day is established at least in part by their mail and any rejection it may bring.

Business reply permits are issued by the U.S. Postal Service. They allow one to send a potential donor, subscriber, or whatever a self-addressed, postage-paid envelope, providing the means for quick, easy response. Pols want donations to return in these business reply envelopes. They spend a great deal of money on consultants who explain how to wring the last penny out of every solicitation, including the specific design of the BREs.

Holders of these business reply permits pay our postal service $75 per year for the permit itself, plus a sort of accounting fee of $185 per annum. The latter fee includes the cost of an assigned bar code printed on the envelopes, which makes it quicker and easier for postal service people to handle the envelopes.

Users of business reply envelopes do not absolutely have to use bar codes. Normally there is a $ .29-per-piece charge for all business reply mail that returns, plus a $ .40-*per-piece* handling fee. If one uses bar codes, however, this handling fee can drop to as little as two cents apiece. Needless to say, most pols use bar codes on their preprinted envelopes. Check some of the many envelopes you receive in the mail to substantiate the fact that business replies are generally bar-coded.

For starters, sting artists can go to party headquarters, county fair booths, or wherever political literature lurks. Pick up as many of these postage-paid envelopes as possible without attracting attention. Use caution and a bit of common sense so that campaign workers do not suspect a rat.

Using a heavy, black magic marker, cover over the bar code strip at the bottom of the envelope. Dump the empty, marker-improved envelope in the mail. Even if the pol's staff has paid accounting fees, it will still cost the campaign $. 29 plus $. 40 cents to take possession of an "empty" envelope.

However, do not actually send the envelope back empty. Place a carefully chosen wad of old newsprint in it so that it seems as though something important is enclosed. Recipients and postal workers must believe that this is a regular BRE, not that a sting is in progress. In a few cases where it was immediately obvious that fraud was involved, some sympathetic postal workers have excused pol's from paying for empty envelopes they received.

It does not do any good to place old nails, sheets of lead, gravel or other heavy waste in the envelopes. Postal clerks will not charge extra for delivery.

It is similarly ineffective to write obscene or suggestive messages on the outside of the envelope. After a few days in the business, staff members become hardened to it all.

Return 100 envelopes and the campaign is out $69—not a great amount but a demoralizing way to spend scarce dollars. Remember to delete the bar codes and to place something in the envelopes so that it is not immediately obvious that they are phony. Also, mail them from a variety of locations around the district.

Problems with BREs became so severe in one western state that postal inspectors were called in. There is some feeling that the inspectors were there simply to appease an irate incumbent, because as far as can be determined, nothing came of the investigation. But anyone deploying this device should assume postal inspectors will be called.

Pros in the industry suggest that business reply envelopes are pretty much doomed as a political device. The only reason they are still extant today is because pols want many small donors listed on their sunshine reports, and the general pub-

Federal Election Laws Require:

_____
(name)

_____
(address)

_____   _____
(city)   (zip)

_____
(telephone number)

_____
(occupation)

_____
(employer or business)

_____
(address of employer or business)

Dear _____ ,
I want to join others in supporting you.

☐ As a volunteer to work with you on your campaign.

☐ With my contribution of:

☐ $5   ☐ $10   ☐ $25   ☐ $50

☐ $100   ☐ Other $ _____ .
(Please enclose check for amount indicated)

(CORPORATE CONTRIBUTIONS ARE PROHIBITED BY FEDERAL LAW.)

Paid for by "_____ for Congress Committee."
A copy of our report is filed with and available from the Federal Election Commission, Washington, D.C.

Dear friends,
    I hope you will join hundreds of Idahoans TODAY in supporting the election of Senator _____ as U.S. Representative from _____ 1st District.
    _____ is a HARD-WORKING and EXPERIENCED lawmaker — native of _____, farm-ranch operator, state senator — in whom we can place TRUST and CONFIDENCE in Washington D.C.
    _____ offers strength and stability. He knows _____, its people, their problems and their needs.
    Now he needs your help.
    Please, without delay, mail your contribution TODAY!

Sincerely,

_____, Finance Chairman
_____ for Congress Committee

P.S. Your Contribution is eligible for a Federal Tax Credit.

A good photocopier and one of these return envelopes used to garner campaign contributions—with a little help from the postal service—are all a monkey wrencher needs to get a good hit on a pol's pocketbook.

lic has only started to use them to sabotage pols. If every business reply envelope operators could get their hands on were returned, the financial impact would be staggering.

    Some political scamsters have expanded on this device dramatically. Cost to print return envelopes in thousand-lot batches is about $125, or about a cent and a quarter each. By using printers located in another state or printers who share similar feelings about pols, some monkey wrenchers have made up thousands of envelopes and dropped them in various mailboxes around the district.

In one case, a determined operator purchased blank envelopes for $75 per thousand. These were the kind that have an extra-large flap that folds all the way over and seals at the bottom edge of the envelope so information can be printed on the inside of the flap. Pols all use stock colors for their envelopes, purchased in bulk. In this instance he didn't even have to go to a printer for help. He ran the blank envelopes through his photocopier, placing the correct address and permit number on them. No message was printed on the inside flap, but no one could tell till it was too late.

Seems strange that so seemingly small amounts of money can have such a tremendous impact on a pol, but they do. A $1,500 to $2,000 hit, at a time when every last dime and then some is committed, makes a big difference.

DISCOURAGING INDIVIDUAL CONTRIBUTORS

Certain types of individuals and businesses are likely to contribute to political campaigns. Consider the effect on the pol if these key people were to receive information that discouraged them from lending their support again.

One can get a feel for who these contributors are in a specific area by securing a copy of a candidate's sunshine report from the secretary of state. In some states, smaller local races for mayor or commissioner are excluded from the state's mandatory filings. Nevertheless, these filings are a good place to start a search for specific names and addresses of contributors. Look for trends in the kinds of individuals and businesses that contribute to a particular pol consistently. Use these names as a starter. Add other like businesses and individuals by looking through the phone book. A few years back it was all the dentists supporting one guy and all the truckers another. These patterns become especially obvious if you go back a few reporting periods.

(Here is another instance where great differences exist between liberals and conservatives. Conservatives generally have nothing to reward voters with after being elected. Liberals usually can be counted on to offer rules and regulations that, in effect, hand businesses who support them a monopoly. Licensing barbers, for instance, is wonderful for existing barbers. It keeps others from getting into the business.)

An operator in North Dakota sent out a special flyer he prepared using stationery store press-on lettering and then Xeroxed them by the hundreds. He said he was an anonymous citizen who lived near the pol and was upset that the candidate ran over his son's new little beagle puppy in his blind haste to get from one place to another to campaign.

In another instance a pol was the victim of the bogus accusation that he wanted to legalize prostitution so his father-in-law could set up legal brothels. This is a crazy scheme, but the pol's father-in-law was very wealthy, and it was done in a state where people half believed it. In retrospect, this was a clever, well-thought-out scam that proved to be effective because it was used against a limited-government candidate.

In times past, charges of bribery in American society were very rare because we were mostly a free country, there being little one could not do if sufficiently skilled. Today, we are a nation of permits and approvals wherein bribery or the charge of such will be believed.

Other ideas include accusing the pol of using illegal drugs when you were with him in college; causing a nasty boat accident that he never acknowledged, although witnesses agreed it was his fault; having a sister who worked making porno flicks; or any other damaging information that may seem applicable to the particular candidate. One former pol was accused of carelessly using bad pesticides on his crops. These accusations do not work when made anonymously to the media, but when released to people on the edge of the campaign, they really get the rumors going.

You could send an anonymous mailing claiming to be a single mom whose teenage daughter worked on the pol's staff. Claim your daughter became pregnant, had to have an abortion at her own expense, and was also stiffed out of her wages and position with the pol. These sorts of charges are common in this day and age. Some may even be true. But most importantly, when they are fed to the proper feminists in the pol's group of supporters, an absolute firestorm will result.

TARGETING PACS

Look very closely at which political action committees have contributed money to the campaign. Do a small amount of research to find out what they expect in return. Usually it is because these PACs want the pol's vote on one of their key issues. Perhaps it's a vote against deregulation of an industry or a vote in favor of more stringent inspections of business rivals. Investigators must use a bit of imagination and creativity to discover why specific people have an interest in the pol.

Send an anonymous note claiming to be a past campaign worker who quit because these issues were near and dear to your heart, but you discovered that the candidate was only using them for his own immediate political advantage. Environmental groups, foresters, farmers, and unions snap right to attention when such accusations are made. At the very least, all of this will waste huge amounts of the pol's time, which will have to be spent straightening things out with his staff and supporters right when time is at a premium. Some political handlers have even noticed a decrease in campaign donations when this type of mailing has been sent out. Doubtful contributors will take a wait-and-see attitude, throwing the pol's budgets in the tub.

Like all of these devices, these notes must be done cleverly, always tailored specifically for the one campaign on which one is working.

WARNING OFF VENDORS

Also look at the candidate's expenditure list for ideas as to where and on what the campaign is spending its money. Send a brief little mimeoed note to all the printers, direct mail marketers, advertising agencies, office managers, photographers, stationery suppliers, and others, saying you are a small businessman who was financially stifled by the candidate. Your experience has been that the pol and his staff are very vindictive and that you cannot divulge your name, but wish to warn others of potential financial dangers. It is often very effective to accuse one of the staff of being a real bandit, allowing the recipient to draw his own conclusion as to why the pol hired this type person. In this case, it is vital to know the staff member's full name and a bit of his history (e.g., where he went to school, where his family lives, etc.).

DIVERTING MAIL

Because campaign staffs are always in a state of flux, one can usually walk into the appropriate post office and cancel the campaign mailings, leaving instructions that all mail be forwarded to the state capital, to someone local who is away on vacation, or to a fictitious address in Washington, D.C. Avoid the temptation to forward the pol's mail to China or Cuba. Postal clerks will never believe you.

Only three or four days will pass before the pol's staff realizes something is amiss and rescinds the forwarding orders. Run this sting about three weeks before election day in the case of political campaigns and just before announcements in the case of sitting pols. Don't cancel mailings at a time when a candidate's business reply envelopes are likely to come flooding in. You would only be saving the campaign money.

While they are at it, especially motivated operators might cancel phone service—perhaps three weeks after cutting the line, also cancel utilities, water, janitorial service, building security, TV cable, or absolutely any other service on which the campaign has come to depend. In one case, just cancellation of TV cable traumatized a pol who wanted to see how an interview went. Just getting this mess untangled cost the staff half a day's work. It was all jolly good fun at the expense of some very deserving people.

6 Providing All the Help Possible

One-year-old political speeches sound absolutely stupid. The context in which they were given has usually vanished, and issues of extreme importance cycle in and out like flotsam on the tide. Items that were once of great importance to people have completely left their minds. Test this theory by listening to a candidate's old campaign speeches from one to four years ago.

Municipal libraries around the country often have copies of political speeches on file. Listeners will be shocked when they discover how out of touch with events various pols sound. Use recordings that are one to four years old. Five-year and older political harangues sound curiously historic; as they get older, they start to sound less and less moronic.

As a result of this syndrome, political animals make quite an industry of looking up old speeches, which they enter by subject matter into computer data banks.

SOWING DISINFORMATION ELECTRONICALLY

More national campaigns are now actually contests of one computer against another. By using extensive data banks, various contenders attempt to keep each other off balance using positions and policies promulgated under last year's political climate. A good example is Ronald Reagan's reference to the Evil Empire early in his campaign. Later, after the Soviets packed up their tent and went home, he was asked about that statement. Reagan was sufficiently popular to get by with simply saying, "That was another time and another place."

Nevertheless, candidates running for office all maintain vast computer data now. Even mayors in small towns make use of computers to keep track of their own and their opponents' positions on issues.

People in the industry talk of breaking computer codes to get into the opposition's data bank, both to see what the opposition has and to plant erroneous information. This should not prove to be terribly difficult for techies who also wish to be political monkey wrenchers. Data banks only work if they are accessible to a pol's many field workers and volunteers. If they can get in using a computer, phone, and modem, so can the outsider who wishes to sow disinformation.

Once in the pol's data bank, one might just change little pieces of information. Changing personal data on his opponents might be enough to cause the pol's data bank users to misquote, losing credibility as well as confidence in their own data bank.

MAKING THE MOST OF
MONOTONOUS MONOLOGUES

A few years back, as I sat listening to a U.S. representative giving a speech to a large convention, it became obvious that monkey wrenchers might use old political harangues themselves as a countermeasure against these old pols. His monologue was an exact duplicate of the campaign speech he used hundreds of times prior to getting elected. (Citizens don't generally realize it, but pols really only have one speech. They tailor the front end by recognizing all of their acquaintances in the crowd and listing all of the nice things

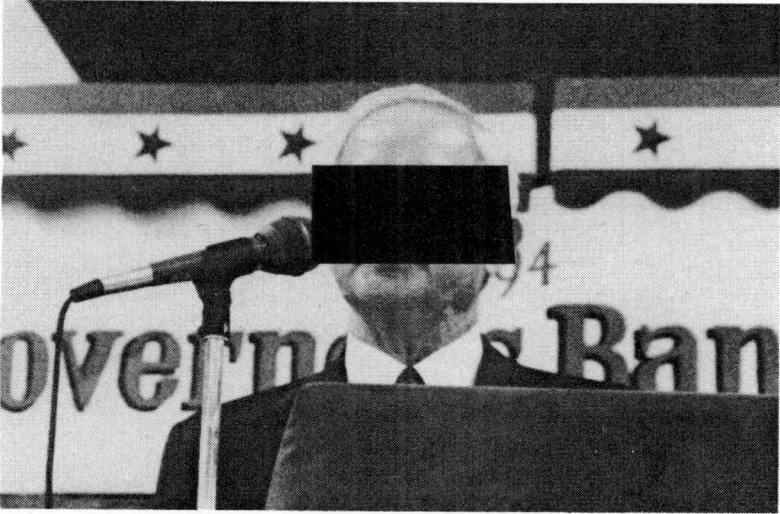

Pols will say anything to win political acclaim.

government has done for the group of people they are
addressing. This listing usually includes several items that
the pol fought tooth and nail but were placed into law over
his objection. If they worked out reasonably well and the
objection was not high-profile, the pol will take credit for
them, even though he originally opposed it. One pol, for
instance, fought welfare reform but later took credit for
money saved as a result of the bill he had ardently opposed
being passed.) At any rate, most of the seasoned rubber
chicken eaters at the conference realized it was last year's
speech with last year's issues. They reacted accordingly. They
were universally turned off and out. A slow cloud of extraneous chatter filled the hall as various people, forced to sit
through the monologues, caught up on gossip. All of this was
very surprising. Basically the same people had sat on the
edge of their chairs and cheered wildly during the same
speech given the year prior.

A political sting activist in Indiana was at a similar meeting. He happened upon an opportunity to secure a large

batch of old campaign tapes, some from the pol's staff and some from the local radio station library. An idea with far-reaching implications popped into the fellow's head.

He rented a very small, simple booth at three or four county fairs that fall. The cost was minimal but, in spite of making arrangements in the name of a small company he set up, he was identified as the perpetrator. He had some very nice signs lettered and hung around the booth. Using nothing more than a boom box with larger external speakers, he played the tapes on a continuous cycle dawn to dusk.

His first reaction was to assume only a handful of people would stop to listen. He resolved to be satisfied with influencing just these folks. However the harangues included some truly outrageous and dated material that ended up attracting modest crowds in some cases.

The targeted pol decided to retire in that case, so it is unclear whether the strategy was actually beneficial. No vote was ever taken.

CREATING CHAOS AT PRESS CONFERENCES

At times it is genuinely tough to tell whether one is doing good or bad. A would-be sting artist posted some nice-looking political flyers made on his laser printer and copy machine in a biker bar in and around Seattle. These posters invited all of the bikers to the pol's news conference announcing his reelection bid. The posters promised free beer and condoms to those who showed up to support the pol. It was the monkey wrencher's assumption that the bikers would show up and disrupt the news conference. He was not a biker himself and did not realize that bikers are actually a civilized lot in their own way.

Many of them came to the news conference, causing—as predicted—a bit of confusion. But the sly dog congressman welcomed them, tailoring his announcement somewhat to the bikers. No free beer and condoms were available, but after asking once, the bikers decided to let the matter drop.

The problem with quick-thinking populist pols is that they will appropriate issues and voters as they encounter them. In this instance, some bikers may have voted for the guy, canceling the negative value their presence should have had in chasing other, more conventional voters away.

STIRRING UP THE MASSES

Taking a cue from a perhaps apocryphal story set in Merrie Olde England, political monkey wrenchers have tried a variety of different advertisement schemes offering to purchase goods and services at inflated rates in the name of the targeted person.

The original tale goes back to the late 1700s when, legend has it, a disgruntled suitor placed an advertisement in a local paper offering an outlandish amount of cash for common alley cats. These were to be brought to the residence where the marriage ceremony of his past flame was to take place. As the tale goes, hundreds brought thousands of cats. Some even brought stray dogs, hoping these would also find a lucrative market.

On finding out all was a hoax, most of these mongrel cats and dogs were turned loose. Bedlam that day in that place was such that the ceremony was cruelly interrupted. Irate people stormed up and down the street, working themselves into a great rage.

This account probably cannot be documented. But it does suggest some interesting possibilities. Why not, for instance, run ads in the free advertising circulars in the pol's name supporting recycling? Claim the pol's commitment is so strong he will purchase all aluminum cans, clean glass, and old newspapers at one-third over the going market rate. Target deserving groups such as scouts, church groups, private schools, and environmental groups as recipients of this largess.

Flyers in supermarkets might encourage people to bring in compost material to add to the campaign's compost pile.

This in itself would be a subject of great comment within that voting district. Other flyers might encourage people to load up all their hazardous waste and bring it to campaign headquarters for disposal.

One could also run ads offering free massage and other "miscellaneous" services, including free car pool coordination, cut-rate taxi service, and free tree trimming, pet neutering, knife sharpening, and any other weird service one's fertile mind could conjure up, listing the pol's office phone as the number to call.

In this case there is no reason to be subtle. The goal is to tie up the pol's office phones with as many irate people as possible. Creating unruly traffic through his office, home, or campaign headquarters is also helpful.

One can envision placing hundreds of preprinted sticky tags offering odd services listing the pol's phone number. Place these out and about in phone booths, johns, bus shelters, public vehicles, and wherever. To the best of my knowledge, this little device has not been tested. People may not call, but then again, they may. One can easily make these tags on a computer using stock purchased from stationery stores. As little as this device costs in time and money, it is certainly worth a try.

ANALYZING VOTING RECORDS FOR PUBLIC SCRUTINY

Phony political analysis of a pol's voting record, leading to a well-publicized rating, has been tried. This is a simple little device that, when used, has caused great trauma among the criminals. It is only effective on incumbents who have been around long enough to vote on a few issues. It is a kind of conglomeration of phony news releases, direct mail, a media scam, and political embarrassment rolled into one package. This is an unlikely one, but when I watched it run, it worked wonderfully well.

We formed a very small ad hoc political action committee

called the "State Friend of the Taxpayer." It was a fairly straight-up effort, but several have been pure fabrication and these were also successful.

We analyzed all of the spending bills on which state legislators voted during a recent session. All that counted was a simple "yes" or "no" vote. We calculated the percentage of the time the pols voted not to spend money. We then tagged those with the highest percentage of "no" votes as Friends of the Taxpayer. No extenuating circumstances were taken into consideration. Nothing but "yes" and "no" votes were tabulated. "Yes" on taxes voters were pilloried for their profligate habits.

We were absolutely amazed. Our little group sent a news release throughout the state. Absolutely *every* newspaper and TV station ran the story. Nobody called to ask how we arrived at the rating or which spending bills were used. State representatives from all over were livid, especially if they were labeled as reckless spenders. Our phones rang off the hook with calls from these people for several days.

Several members of the original core group expanded on the idea, using it for purely sting-type publicity. One man devised a letterhead for a nonexistent environmental group. He did a phony rating on environmental legislation, ranking some liberals very low and some conservatives very high. This got everyone in trouble with their constituencies. Most of the papers in the region carried that "news."

Another group rated liberals on their pro-banker voting record. Here is a rating based on pols who talk one way and vote the other, their news release stated.

In one case, conservative pols were ranked by IQ or the IQs of their staff. Of course, there was no way to come up with valid IQ scores on these guys. Lobbyists were quoted as the source of information on IQs.

Thankfully, it is virtually impossible to describe all of the happy consternation these ratings caused. Editorials were written, people complained, pols spent time and money explaining things, and it appeared that several candidates might have lost elections at least in part because of this negative publicity.

As a final irony, some of the pols began to quote the rating results in some of their speeches. Had this trend become widespread, we were prepared to put out another release claiming the first was entirely phony.

Aside from some discomfort experienced by thieves, a great time was had by all.

7 The Pol's Vehicle

Knowing which vehicle the pol is using or driving and/or the make, model, and license number of staff members' vehicles is of great benefit. Anytime you spot a vehicle in which accomplices of the pol can be seen, jot down its vital statistics. These are the vehicles used to transport the pol to news conferences, luncheons, and rallies. Obviously, they must come and go and must remain somewhat near while the pol does his business.

Staff members usually drive vehicles plastered over with signs, lights, and bumper stickers. Incumbents often use nice, clean late-model vehicles donated to the office by wealthy supporters. These will not be defaced with signs and stickers. If all else fails, one can learn about vehicle donors by looking at appropriate sunshine reports at the secretary of state's office. These reports should list all donors of everything to the campaign. They may also reveal the fact that the pol has signed over several of his own or his wife's vehicles to the campaign.

Incumbents usually keep residences far away from their districts, but challengers will have houses (homes) past which one could drive in search of vehicle information.

A pol inconsistently dedicates a new road he opposed. Rather than arguing with him in the media, make sure his car never arrives at the ceremony.

Drive by early in the morning to check. Verify license numbers, models, and makes with the state vehicle licensing office. In all states that I know of, this information is part of the public record.

At times it is possible to verify names of campaign staffers by way of license plate numbers taken from vehicles spotted at the scene of the crime. Ideas for monkey wrenching these vehicles range from the ridiculous to the sublime.

An attorney, knowing that this book was in process, told me about the instance when he attended a League of Women Voters political forum while still in school. Halfway through he became so disgusted that he walked out to the parking lot and pulled the stem cores on all the cars' tires. Undoubtedly, he got a number of innocent people and did very little to permanently slow or cost the assembled pols.

Better to rig up the pol's vehicles so that it permanently breaks down, forcing the pol to miss appointments and pay expensive repair, tow, and garage bills. It is especially laudatory if these events occur in out-of-the-way places where returning to pick up the repaired vehicle is difficult.

Probably the best tried-and-true method of thoroughly killing a gasoline engine is to place common naphthalene (moth balls) in the gas tank. Considerably more are required than one would first suppose, and they take time to dissolve, especially if the tank is only half full. Driving on a smooth superhighway also is not conducive to mixing gasoline and mothballs, which makes the period between insertion and engine seize-up even longer.

After two cups of moth balls dissolve in the fuel, they cause the engine to begin to race and then to blow clouds of black smoke. If the tank is not immediately pumped dry and new, clean fuel added, the engine will heat, carbon up, and seize. Mechanics who have worked on engines so treated claim that generally the entire power plant is gunny-bagged, including the block.

Let's assume one has the pol's vehicle in sight along with two or three belonging to staff members, and—tragedy of tragedies—no moth balls are at hand.

Do not be discouraged; another, equally effective, simple expedient can be used. Common packing peanuts or any Styrofoam sufficiently crushed to pass into the gas tank through the filler nozzle are just as effective for killing a gasoline engine. Like moth balls, it takes far more Styrofoam than one could initially suppose. Most experts recommend at least two large handfuls per tank of gasoline.

Glass marbles rolling around in a gas tank can drive some people to distraction. They are impossible to get out without removing the fuel tank, which can be quite expensive.

If you can find a live chicken and access the interior of the pol's auto unseen, shut it in the pol's vehicle. We did this as kids on the farm. Anyone's car so treated will never be usable again. In an hour the odor becomes unimaginably bad.

In Ohio, an especially irate citizen threw a chain on a pol's car and pulled it off down the road with his four-wheel-drive

Aspiring pols find they must campaign in odd places. Someone could pull the plug on this boat as it steams upriver, stranding and embarrassing a toothy political thief.

truck. He left it at a secluded spot about three miles away. A farmer eventually found the pol's car, and the pol received some interesting press.

One pol started to ride a bicycle around the district as part of his campaign. Some kids stole it, which was a dumb idea. Better he was out in the boonies pumping his wheel than someplace important getting votes.

Many pols use campaign buses. They know these are vulnerable, so they post guards around them at all times. Best to be very careful when moving against a campaign bus or van.

One device that is difficult to arrange, but which is very effective if one can pull it off, is to arrange for the pol to somehow damage the property of another. These incidents actually happen from time to time but are not generally reported by the media. Their advantage is that they get thrown into the rumor mill in the district, especially if orchestrated well before the election.

Consider throwing a pol or staffer's car out of gear on a hilly parking area so that it crashes into other parked vehicles. If it works, call all of the media you can think of quickly.

A drum of some substance with the businessman candidate's company name on it might be discovered someplace in an alley behind a school or wherever. It may just be a blue plastic drum as available from many surplus stores, stenciled with the fellow's company name. Partly filled with a few gallons of old engine oil, it will look really bad. Keep this from getting swept under the rug by calling the local media with an anonymous tip. Simply put the pol's firm name in place of the original business name on the drum. Testing alone to determine what is in the barrel will cost the pol a bundle.

At a time when I worked on a politician's staff, someone poked toothpicks in all of the staff car locks. They were broken off clean, making removal difficult. We were running only an hour late after purchasing needle-nose pliers to get one splinter out of one lock. During the next speech we cleaned all of the remaining locks. Had the monkey wrencher also squirted a bit of super glue into the locks, our campaign would have been stalled for the better part of a week. At the time we were really out in the boonies.

8 Fighting Organized Crime

Political monkey wrenchers, or groups they have formed, who will not suffer unduly as a result of stepping out into the spotlight, can try running a "Dumbest Congressman" contest.

Originally conceived and implemented by some good-old-boy Southern Dixiecrats, this device, which takes the form of a contest, has lots of potential for political embarrassment. This terribly effective device likely will draw great media attention, which may be directed at one or two individuals. It is a ploy best run by an established group rather than lone citizens.

On the upside, any group—no matter how small or previously inconspicuous—could conceivably use it to garner national publicity. Information accumulated from the contest is a treasure trove, useful for future political monkey wrenching.

The extent of media coverage depends on one's ability to talk in front of cameras, write news releases, and generally push media hot buttons. Best success seems to come when a previously nonpartisan group takes a "pox on all your houses" approach, going after everyone, regardless of party affiliation.

The southern group that originally thought up and implemented this device were somewhat constrained by their desire to protect preconceived friends while exposing those thought to be scalawags. They were unwilling to be even handedly arbitrary, at least in a public sense. These are times in the United States when compromise, appeasement, and lack of standards give the appearance of brilliance to some citizens.

But contest organizers could have easily and quickly passed over comments about friends without making a big deal out of it. Or they could have rethought their position regarding all politicians in general.

Basically, organizers offer a rich reward to the individual who, in 100 words or less, best articulates the contest premise, "My congressman/woman is the dumbest in Washington, D.C., because . . ." For the media's sake, this is shortened to the Dumbest Congressman contest.

The best entry, to be determined by a panel of judges, must win an award sufficient to catch people's attention. Probably no less than $500 or $1,000 would work. This sounds like a great deal of money for a group or individual to raise, but again, our mendacious government comes to the rescue—in this case, to its own disadvantage.

Instead of offering $500 in cash, offer a $500 government savings bond. These bonds cost exactly half their face value. In the case of a $500 bond, cash cost is $250!

Federal judges have ruled that it is perfectly legal to advertise a $500 bond when, in fact, it cost only $250 and can probably not even be immediately cashed for this price. In this regard, government bonds make wonderful, if somewhat devious, contest awards. Some contest participants may discover that government bonds are not worth what the government says they are. But one can view this discovery as being an ancillary benefit rather than one of the principal goals of the contest.

Well-written contest rules must be developed, including who can or cannot participate, how one participates, how winners will be determined, when they will be selected, and how winners will be notified. Opening the contest to the widest possible group of participants seems desirable.

The good old boys who organized the first contest stipulated that people could only write about the senators and representatives ruling the area in which they currently resided. Participants could enter as often as they could write up 100-word essays, but anything more than 100 words was summarily rejected. Organizers intentionally left the rules as simple as possible. They included a last postmark date and the fact that the statement had to be signed and addressed. They did not include suggestions or provide a sense of direction for participants. This was, perhaps, the loss of a golden opportunity. By offering a sample, or model, they could have set out the level of stridency judges would likely find appropriate.

Consider the following "sample" that could have been included with contest instructions:

My senator, Sen. Sam Snort, District 3, Kentucky, is so dumb he honestly believes he can bribe me using my own money. If Snort truly understood the true nature of his chosen occupation, he would admit that he is living on the fruits of common theft.

Webster defines theft as the involuntary, forcible conversion of one's personal property to the use and control of another. When Snort voted to increase taxes, he voted to increase theft in the land. Snort is not smart enough to see that a nation of thieves cannot long endure.

Snort is so dumb he commonly advocates government schools that have never worked here or any other place in the world. He is so dumb he seems to believe none of his constituents travel and read.

Snort's selection of a wife mirrors his stupidity. Those doubting this premise need only speak with her a few seconds before realizing she is the original airhead with no socially redeeming qualities or original thoughts.

Snort's association with known criminals in Washington, D.C., some of whom are under indictment or already in jail, suggests poor judgment pushed by an extremely low IQ.

Because of Snort's criminal record, his known associates, and his malicious ignorance of history, he certainly deserves the title of stupidest man in Congress.

Something like this example is bound to get people in the correct frame of mind.

One possibility the contest holds is that of some obscure citizen uncovering or revealing some actual, documentable dishonesties or indiscretions on the part of his pol. Alert contest organizers could parlay these facts into real advantages.

The first hurdle is deciding to do the project. Next, one must raise sufficient money to catch the attention of potential contest participants. This is sometimes tough, but it is made somewhat easier by the use of a government bond scam. Then one must write up contest rules. Do this as easily as possible by plagiarizing rules used by McDonald's, Publisher's Clearing House, a grocery chain, or whatever. Run a draft of the rules past an attorney to be sure they are not blatantly illegal. Print up the rules and regulations, including the post office box to which all responses must be sent.

Include a sample response on the original printed material if it seems that this will stimulate creative juices.

The last task involves something of an art rather than a skill. Success will only come if one is good to very good at generating publicity for the event. There must be news conferences, mailings, news releases, TV appearances, interviews with evening news people (who will be less than thrilled about this contest), and then continuing ongoing publicity as the contest unfolds. One brief shot on the evening news will not generate enough enthusiasm to carry 30 to 60 days of contest life.

One especially sage political manipulator suggested running the contest in conjunction with other conventional events. These could include a booth at the county or state fair, yuppie events in the park, rock concerts, craft sales, farmers' markets, and any other widely attended public gatherings. Just showing up with such an outrageous promotion could guarantee sufficient publicity to make it very successful.

9 Other Good Ideas

It is sometimes amazing to me how many people share a similar visceral dislike for American politicians.

A fellow in Sitka, Alaska, on hearing that this volume was in process, called on his own nickel to tell me about a political sting he thought was especially laudatory.

PHONE SCAMS

Seems a pol in his area ran his campaign and his legislative offices out of the local offices of a far left religious organization. On its face, the move was logical and even legal. Sitka is so remote, small, and cut off that neither a legislative office nor a campaign office, normally required to whip up the achievements of the pol in the eyes of constituents, could be justified.

But, as this monkey wrencher pointed out, when running stings on pols one should always keep in mind the distinction between personal and campaign expenditures that the pol must raise and cash that the U.S. government pays for local legislative offices that all national pols are allowed to maintain. In other words, running up a pol's bills in his local official office does nothing but increase tax liabilities for our children because the government pays the bill. Money to run government is mostly derived from government debt, which must be paid in the future. So hit them in their own pockets, not in a pocket funded by taxpayers' money.

At any rate, the fellow easily accessed the phone line switch box behind the offending pol's office. Instead of tapping the phone, our friend surreptitiously connected a $7.99 Wal-Mart phone directly into the office line. It was a very simple operation performed mostly by trial and error till he got a dial tone. A call to his wife—which she responded to by calling the pol's number—confirmed that he had accessed the line of the far left religious organization that was actually fronting for the pol's campaign organization, not his local legislative office. Not black bag, but not bad for amateurs.

The fellow then dialed 00 because the office was on Sprint/MCI. If it had been on the AT&T system, he would have dialed 0 to reach an international operator. No need to sleuth this one out, either. Just dial any operator, give him the office number, and he will tell you whether you have the correct long-distance carrier.

Once you have the international operator on the line, ask for an English-speaking operator in Tokyo. The cost to the office for just this connection is about $4. You could also try Paris, Bangkok, or Cairo, but efficiency in Japan is appropriately high, and costs are as great as anyone can reasonably find.

Ask for the number of the time operator in Tokyo. This is a repetitive recording that runs as long as the phone remains connected with it. The billing rate is about $2.50 for the first minute and $1 thereafter.

The numbers for reaching Tokyo will be as follows: 011 = international access, 81 = country code, 3 = Tokyo city code. Dial this plus the number of the time recording as obtained from the international operator.

Our friend, the monkey wrencher, let the phone sit on Tokyo time from Friday night at 7:30 p.m. till 5:30 a.m. Monday when, on his way to work, he drove up the alley to remove the device. Total bill was about 58 hours at $60 per hour, or $3,480! It was enough that the incident made the papers, the fellow claims.

Needless to say, this sort of bill virtually destroyed the pol's shell campaign organization. Some long-distance carriers will excuse charges for domestic phone scams, but, where transfer fees are involved, international carriers are hard-nosed about such forgiveness.

In another pol's office in Washington state, a staffer actually ran up $1,200 in calls to a 900 porn line. This proved to be a wonderful case of shooting oneself in the foot, as the pol had to pay up lest bad publicity overwhelm the organization. Attempts were made to get the funds out of the offending staffer, but it proved to be a case of trying to get blood out of a stone and all of that.

Why not, one could validly ask, tap into a pol's personal line and call one of the porn outfits that features a 900 number with a continuous recording? These lines usually bill out at about $2.50 per minute, indicating that a phone connected over a weekend might rack up well over five grand in charges. A three-day weekend hookup could end up being a real whizzer!

IRS STINGS

Taxes and intense dislike of them often come to people's minds. Why can't the pols be subject to the same trauma we are relative to paying them? "Perhaps turning the pol in on one of the IRS snitch lines might be laudable," well-meaning citizens often suggest.

It can be done, and it probably has been done with some measure of success. But it ain't as easy as it sounds. Each taxing district has its own policy regarding tax snitches. Generally, the IRS requires that a name be tied to any information it acts on. That, in part, is why they offer 10 percent of any unpaid taxes they are able to collect as a result of the snitch's information as a reward.

You can find out about snitch lines in your own IRS district anonymously by calling the IRS 800 information number listed in the telephone directory. Simply ask if this type of office is available and whom, at what number, you should call. Most IRS district offices have a few people whose main duty is to assess the political ramifications of going after high-profile people, including pols. U.S. senators or representatives who sit on powerful committees *will not* be harassed by the IRS, even if the story one provides is really plausible. On the other hand, pols who have criticized the IRS in the past will be quickly singled out for a detailed audit in a most unmerciful manner.

Any information one "assembles" and provides to the IRS anonymously must initially sound very plausible to the IRS, or it will not even spend one minute looking into it.

One can always plausibly accuse the pol of taking walking around money. This is cash stuffed in his pocket or slipped via an envelope into a briefcase. Sometimes walking around money is in the form of rolls of stamps. All pols take this sort of campaign contribution, and the IRS knows it. It won't act on the tip unless it has a rock-solid witness who will come forward to substantiate these charges and appear in tax court in support of them.

In summary, one could possibly orchestrate an IRS sting on a pol, but to be successful it would have to be very well thought out, reflecting a great deal of in-depth knowledge of the pol and his operation, his life-style, his outside business-es, hobbies, and other activities. One would have to conclude that if they knew that much about a person, other simpler methods of attack would be evident.

HOW OTHER BUREAUCRATS CAN BE OF HELP

This is not to say that pols cannot be attacked through

other governmental agencies, many of which can cause intense grief. Current news is full of items concerning people who have filed complaints with the Human Rights Commission, OSHA, EPA, Customs, BATF, DEA, and even the Office of Immigration and Naturalization. In this last case alone, the family of a pol was forced to pay $250,000 in fines over some carefully planned but phony charges relative to family business hiring practices.

If one can get its attention, the Drug Enforcement Agency has absolute dictatorial power. They can summarily search anyone, as well as seize of any cash the person happens to be carrying. Attempts, even through legal proceedings, to get the cash returned always fail. DEA people arbitrarily seize vehicles, boats, cameras, houses, bank accounts, office furniture, computers, or whatever one has of value. Once seized it is never returned, although this has not yet been tested in the case of pols.

Try to alert the DEA if you suspect a pol (especially a nonincumbent) is traveling with more than $500 in cash. You might also try planting a small amount of illegal drugs on the candidate—or easier, on a staff member. Call the DEA and anonymously report that a specific staff member is packing drugs. Many staff members are relatively young, adding to the plausibility of this sort of sting.

Appearing credible in the eyes of other government agencies requires that one have an extremely well thought through, plausible, possible, realistic tale to tell. Obviously, if one looks at current charges as reported in the news, these accusations do not have to be true. They do, however, have to meld well with current political expectations and catch the fancy of the public at large.

Sexual harassment charges are, at this writing, pretty trendy. Having an office building with asbestos is not terribly trendy, although, reported to the correct agency, this could be costly for the pol.

None of these devices should be laid aside cavalierly simply because no exact road map for their use exists. Sitting politicians spend a great deal of time each day trying to devise valid plans wherein another agency can be induced to do their dirty work attacking a sitting opponent.

MAKING A MESS OF THINGS

This last true incident will close this volume of ideas as to how ordinary peon types might retaliate against criminals who always promise much to those not wise enough to know that in order to give, one must forcibly take from the other guy. Again, this is a true account of a little sting, but even the city wherein it occurred must remain anonymous.

Two especially fed-up monkey wrenchers discovered a public john in the building in which a pol had his office. It wasn't easy to find or very well marked, but it was there for use by staff members. On several occasions they plugged the john up tight with old newspapers. But this was only a minor inconvenience that cost the pol nothing to remedy.

Next our two heroes flushed two old-fashioned silver salute firecrackers down the stool. When they detonated they cracked the cast-iron pipe in the floor below. People, mostly from the pol's office, continued to use the facility, creating a horrible mess. Finally the landlord had enough—he asked the pol to leave before bigger and better things happened to his office building.

It was a wise move. For their next act they planned to catch a live owl or a skunk and turn it loose in the pol's office. Under the circumstances, either would have been fairly easy to pull off as well as very appropriate.

PLANTING A PIECE ON THE POL

I asked an old, retired, rehabilitated pol about slipping a cheap pistol in the bag of a senator or representative's bag on the way back to D.C. My plan was to call anonymously, reporting that the fellow had an illegal pistol in the district.

"Won't work," the pol said. "These guys grant themselves

immunity. Nobody else in D.C. can own a firearm, but they can." Seems like the same old song—they can steal from us but the laws are structured to protect their theft.

Conclusion

Many of the people who contributed to this manual are already in the business of political monkey wrenching. I met them during my brief sojourn into this odd world of making democracy work. These are paid professionals working for pols who hire them specifically to sit around thinking this sort of stuff up.

They will, perhaps, be surprised to find all of this material summarized into one volume. It may be even more surprising for many of them to discover what some really fed-up amateurs are doing.

Now average citizens who feel genuinely threatened and subjugated by pols have a few valid methods of retaliation open to them. There may be comfort in just knowing these devices are available, even if one elects not to use them. Please keep in mind that when paid professionals run these stings, their first move is to collect absolutely everything on and about the target possible. Then they hit the pol in a place where it really hurts, not at a place where he simply forwards the bill on to the government or assigns a staffer to handle it.

Always, one must be intensely clever. Being so, a monkey wrencher must decide whether it is best to publicly acknowledge his role or remain in the background. To an extent it does not matter, as pols expect the unexpected and will not be particularly surprised when they are the target of a sting. Their problem will be figuring out why they are getting hit from so many different places at once.

The reader's problem, if he chooses to give up his status as an anonymous monkey wrencher, is that he may himself be hit by some very sophisticated stings orchestrated by irate pols. Bear in mind that when a pol or his staff member calls the DEA or IRS, these agencies listen. Some pols hit back very hard and very professionally in an attempt to minimize the amount of grief with which they must contend.

Nevertheless, one could easily envision some of the big-time fascists being hit by many, many angry citizens at the same time. These stings, all done in retaliation for cavalier disregard of our most cherished constitutional rights, could come so fast and furious that political disaster would be inevitable.

Given the fact that more people will be thinking about this subject, some new, very clever, very effective devices could surface. I personally look forward to reading about them in the papers.

It doesn't matter who gets caught in the web. Shakespeare summed it up nicely when he wrote, "A pox on all their houses—they are all a pack of thieves."